PELICAN BOOK A836

Victorian Architecture

Robert Furneaux Jordan was born in 1905 and educated at King Edward's School, Birmingham, and the Birmingham School of Art. He became an Associate of the R.I.B.A. and received his A.A. Diploma in 1928 from The Architectural Association school in London. He lectured on design and architectural history there from 1934 to 1963, while at the same time in general practice as an architect. In 1948 he became the school's Principal, leaving in 1951 for the position of Architectural Correspondent to the *Observer*, which he held for the next ten years. After this he was Hoffmann-Wood Professor of Architecture in the University of Leeds, 1961–2, and visiting Professor of Architecture in the University of Syracuse, U.S.A.

Robert Jordan has been a frequent broadcaster on the B.B.C. and has contributed to architectural journals. He is the author of *The English House* (1959), and *European Architecture* (1961). He has lived mainly in London but is now married and lives in Wiltshire, with interests ranging from the field of ideas and cultures to racial freedom and liberalism. He has also written a successful detective story under a *nom de plume*.

Victorian Architecture

Robert Furneaux Jordan

PENGUIN BOOKS

Penguin Books Ltd, Harmondsworth, Middlesex, England
Penguin Books Inc., 3300 Clipper Mill Road, Baltimore 11, Md, U.S.A.
Penguin Books Pty Ltd, Ringwood, Victoria, Australia

First published 1966
Copyright © Robert Furneaux Jordan, 1966

Designed by Gerald Cinamon
Made and printed in Great Britain by Jarrold and Sons Ltd, Norwich
Set in Monotype Scotch Roman

To Eira

Contents

List of Illustrations   9

Preface   15

Acknowledgements   21

1   *The Nature of an Industrial Revolution*   25

2   *The Nature of a Romantic Movement*   42

3   *The Gothic Revival: Phase One*   58

4   *The Gothic Revival: Phase Two*   77

5   *The Crystal Palace and the Engineers*   110

6   *High Victorianism*   136

7   *Ruskin and Morris*   170

8   *Arts and Crafts, and* Art Nouveau   185

9   *The House*   206

10   *Modernity is Born*   240

Bibliography   263

Index   269

List of Illustrations

	T. E. Knightley: Birkbeck Bank, Chancery Lane, London, 1895–6	22
1	Abraham Darby: Coalbrookdale Bridge, Shropshire, 1779	28
2	Stockport Viaduct and Canal, mid nineteenth century	30
3	Jesse Hartley: Albert Docks, Liverpool, 1850	31
4	Air view, Tower Bridge, London, 1895	32
5	Speculative housing, Addison Road, Kensington, London, 1840	33
6	Portrait, Isambard Kingdom Brunel, 1806–59	36
7	I. K. Brunel: Royal Albert Bridge, Saltash, Plymouth, 1859	37
8	Warehouses, Manchester, mid nineteenth century	38
9	Thomas Telford: St Katherine's Dock, London, 1824–8	38
10	Carriages in Hyde Park, London	40
11	Wandsworth Prison, London	41
12	Queen Victoria's drawing-room, Osborne House	43
13	John Martin: *The Great Day of His Wrath*	49
14	Air view, Buckingham Palace and St James's	53
15	John Nash: Blaise Hamlet, near Bristol, 1811	54
16	Christopher Wren: St Mary, Aldermary, London, 1704	61
17	Robert Adam *et al.*: Strawberry Hill, Twickenham, exterior, 1753	64
18	Robert Adam *et al.*: Strawberry Hill, Twickenham, the library, 1753	65
19	Sanderson Miller: Sham ruin, Hagley, Worcestershire, 1748	66
20	R. Bentley: Frontispiece to Gray's 'Elegy', 1753	67
21	James Wyatt: Belvoir Castle, Leicestershire, begun 1800	69
22	James Wyatt: Fonthill Abbey, Wiltshire, central octagon, 1796–9	70
23	James Wyatt: Fonthill Abbey, Wiltshire, view from the park, 1796–9	70
24	James Savage: St Luke's, Chelsea, London, 1820	73

25	Charles Barry and A.W.N.Pugin: Houses of Parliament, London, 1836–45	75
26	A.W.N.Pugin: *Apology for the Revival of Christian Architecture in England*, frontispiece, 1843	77
27	A.W.N.Pugin: Scarisbrick Hall, Southport, Lancashire, exterior, 1837	79
28	A.W.N.Pugin: Scarisbrick Hall, Southport, Lancashire, red drawing-room, 1837	80
29	A.W.N.Pugin: St Chad's Cathedral, Birmingham, 1839	82
30	A.W.N.Pugin: Alton Towers, Staffordshire, 1847	83
31	Charles Barry and A.W.N.Pugin: Houses of Parliament, London, St Stephen's Chapel, 1836–45	84
32	Charles Barry and A.W.N.Pugin: Houses of Parliament, London, Royal Gallery, 1836–45	85
33	Charles Barry and A.W.N.Pugin: Houses of Parliament, London, main staircase, 1836–45	86
34	Charles Barry and A.W.N.Pugin: Houses of Parliament, London, view from Henry vii's Chapel, 1836–45	87
35	W.Butterfield: All Saint's, Margaret Street, London, 1849–59	88
36	W.Butterfield: Keble College Chapel, Oxford, 1873	90
37	W.Butterfield: St Saviour's Vicarage, Coalpit Heath, Gloucestershire, 1844	91
38	Gilbert Scott: Albert Memorial, London, 1864	95
39	Gilbert Scott: St Pancras Hotel, London, 1865	96
40	G.E.Street: Royal Courts of Justice, London, the Strand front, 1871–82	99
41	G.E.Street: Royal Courts of Justice, London, the Carey Street front, 1871–82	100
42	G.E.Street: Royal Courts of Justice, London, the Great Hall, 1871–82	101
43	W.Burges: Cardiff Castle, the hall, 1865–81	103
44	W.Burges: Cardiff Castle, the main stair, 1865–81	104
45	G.M.Kemp: Scott Memorial, Princes Street, Edinburgh, 1840	106
46	Dèane and Woodward: University Museum, Oxford, 1855–9	106
47	J.L.Pearson: St Augustine's, Kilburn, London, 1870–80	107
48	T.G.Jackson: Brasenose College, Oxford	107
49	G.F.Bodley: Church at Hoar Cross, Staffordshire, 1873	108
50	J.L.Pearson: The Cathedral, Truro, begun 1880	108

51   Ninian Comper: St Cyprian's, Clarence Gate, London,
       chancel screen, 1903   109

52   Ford Madox Brown: *Work*, 1852–65   112

53   Speculative building, Newcastle on Tyne, workers' cottages,
       mid nineteenth century   114

54   W.Cubitt: Mimram Viaduct, Welwyn, Hertfordshire, 1846   117

55   Robert Stephenson: Britannia Bridge, Menai Strait, 1845–50   118

56   W.P.Frith: *The Railway Station* (Paddington), 1862   119

57   J.Hawkshaw: Cannon Street Station, London, 1865   120

58   Queen Victoria's Saloon on the Royal Train   121

59   V.Bazalgette: Victoria Embankment, London, 1864–70   122

60   J.Paxton: Crystal Palace, London, view from Hyde Park, 1851   123

61   J.Paxton: Crystal Palace, London,
       general view of interior, 1851   124

62   J.Paxton: Crystal Palace, London, west nave
       and transept, 1851   125

63   Decimus Burton and Richard Turner: The Palm House, Kew,
       London, 1845   127

64   W.H.Barlow and R.M.Ordish: St Pancras Station, London, 1863   128

65   J.Paxton: Crystal Palace, London, blotting paper sketch
       and telegram, 1850   129

66   Lewis Cubitt: King's Cross Station, London, 1851–2   132

67   J.B.Bunning: The Coal Exchange, London, 1846–9   133

68   Deane and Woodward: University Museum, Oxford, 1855–9   134

69   John Nash: Cumberland Terrace, Regent's Park, London, 1826   139

70   H.L.Elmes and C.R.Cockerell: St George's Hall, Liverpool,
       1837–54   140

71   C.R.Cockerell: St George's Hall, Liverpool,
       Concert Hall, *c.* 1850   141

72   J.Young: Eaton Square, London, 1826   142

73   R.Smirke: British Museum, London, 1823–47   144

74   C.R.Cockerell: Bank of England, Liverpool, 1845   145

75   Air view, Admiralty Arch and Trafalgar Square, London   146

76   P.Hardwick: Euston Station, London, the Doric Propylaea, 1847   147

77   Alexander Thomson: Caledonian Road Free Church, Glasgow, 1856   149

78   Thomas Hamilton: High School, Edinburgh, 1825   150

79   Alexander Thomson: Moray Place, Glasgow, 1859   151

80	Cuthbert Brodrick: Grand Hotel, Scarborough, 1863	154
81	John Giles: Langham Hotel, Portland Place, London, 1864	155
82	Cuthbert Brodrick: The Town Hall, Leeds, 1855–9	156
83	W. Young: City Chambers, Glasgow, 1889	157
84	Alfred Waterhouse: Assize Court, Manchester, 1859–64	158
85	Alfred Waterhouse: The Town Hall, Manchester, 1868–77	159
86	London County Council Architect's Department: Flats, Millbank, London, 1897	160
87	Air view, South Kensington, London	161
88	Francis Fowke: Victoria and Albert Museum, Kensington, London, courtyard, 1866	162
89	H. Gribble: Brompton Oratory, Kensington, London, 1888–97	163
90	T. E. Colcutt: Imperial Institute, Kensington, London, 1887–93	165
91	View towards Ludgate Hill, City of London	166
92	Gilbert Scott: Foreign Office, London, 1862–75	167
93	Highgate Cemetery, London, the Columbarium	168
94	John Everett Millais: *Portrait of John Ruskin*, 1853	173
95	Philip Webb: The Red House, Bexley Heath, Kent, 1859	179
96	William Morris: 'Compton' chintz, 1896	181
97	William Morris: The settle at the Red House, 1859	182
98	Philip Webb: Clouds, Wiltshire, drawing-room, 1877–86	183
99	Ernest Gimson: Lea Cottage, Markfield, Charnwood Forest, Leicestershire, c. 1900	188
100	Ernest Gimson: Dining-room chairs, 1901	190
101	Ernest Gimson: A chest, 1901	191
102	Ernest Gimson: The White House, Leicester, 1897	192
103	C. F. A. Voysey: House at Shackleford, Surrey, 1897	193
104	C. F. A. Voysey: The Homestead, Frinton, Essex, 1905	194
105	Bruce Talbert: Design for an interior, 1890	195
106	George Walton: The Leys, Elstree, Hertfordshire, billiard room, 1901	196
107	C. R. Mackintosh: 120 Main Street, Glasgow, the drawing-room, 1900	200
108	C. R. Mackintosh: Tea room, Ingram Street, Glasgow, 1907	202
109	C. R. Mackintosh: The Art School, Glasgow, library, 1907	204
110	C. R. Mackintosh: The Art School, Glasgow, entrance, 1898	205
111	M. D. Wyatt: Alford House, Kensington, London, 1872	212
112	Thomas Cubitt: Osborne House, Isle of Wight, 1845	212

113   Upholsterer's catalogue: Grand piano in the 'Gothic Style'   214

114   William Smith: Balmoral House, Aberdeenshire, 1853   215

115   W. H. Crossland: Royal Holloway College, Egham, Surrey, 1879   217

116   W. H. Crossland: Royal Holloway College, Egham, Surrey, detail of tower, 1879   218

117   John Nash, Edward Blore *et al.*: Buckingham Palace, London, the Bow Library, 1821–47   220

118   Charles Barry: Trentham Hall, Staffordshire, 1851   221

119   Alfred Waterhouse: Eaton Hall, Cheshire, 1867–80   222

120   Alfred Waterhouse: Eaton Hall, Cheshire, main stair, 1867–80   223

121   R. Norman Shaw: Cragside, Rothbury, Northumberland, 1870   225

122   R. Norman Shaw: Dawpool, Birkenhead, Cheshire, 1882   227

123   R. Norman Shaw: 185 Queen's Gate, Kensington, London, 1890   228

124   R. Norman Shaw: New Zealand Chambers, Leadenhall Street, London, 1872–4   229

125   R. Norman Shaw: Swan House, Chelsea, London, 1876   230

126   R. Norman Shaw: Piccadilly Hotel, London, 1905   231

127   R. Norman Shaw: Bryanston, Blandford, Dorset, 1890   232

128   Edwin Lutyens: Munstead Wood, Surrey, 1896   235

129   Speculative housing, 81 Banbury Road, Oxford, mid nineteenth century   236

130   Model housing, Sycamore Road, Bournville Estate, begun 1895   238

131   Philanthropic housing, flats for Peabody Trust, Holborn, London, *c.* 1880.   239

132   The Admiralty: Boat Shed, Sheerness, Kent   242

133   Peter Behrens: A.E.G. Turbine Factory, Berlin, 1909   245

134   Walter Gropius and Adolf Meyer: Fagus Factory, Alfeld, Germany, 1911   246

135   Walter Gropius and Adolf Meyer: Werkbund Exhibition Factory, Cologne, 1914   249

136   H. H. Richardson: Marshall Field Store, Chicago, 1885–7   253

137   Dankmar Adler and Louis Sullivan: Auditorium Building, Chicago, 1887–9   254

138   Louis Sullivan: Carson Pirie Scott Store, Chicago, 1899–1903   257

139   Dankmar Adler and Louis Sullivan: Guaranty Building, Chicago, 1894–5   259

Preface

We live in an age not of great art but of great scholarship. Everything is collected, dated and catalogued. So far as Victorian architecture is concerned we have now passed from the esoteric to the popular. To be interested is no longer to be considered odd. We all owe an incalculable debt to the late Mr Goodhart-Rendel who was a pioneer of Victorian research at a time when the subject was not only esoteric but beyond the pale. Kenneth Clark's *Gothic Revival*, published in 1928, opened the first window upon an episode in the history of taste that was then still despised. Professor Pevsner's *Pioneers of the Modern Movement* was a classic from the moment that it appeared in 1936 – the first attempt to build a bridge between the Victorian Age and modern architecture. If Professor Russell Hitchcock's *Architecture of the Nineteenth and Twentieth Centuries* (1958) shows too little understanding of the social and technical roots of English Victorianism, it remains a most comprehensive work of reference. To all these, and to innumerable others, any writer on Victorian architecture must acknowledge a debt. At the same time my object is quite different from theirs.

The years of cataloguing and annotating are over. Comprehension must now replace erudition. The 'how' and the 'where' have been dealt with, not so the 'why'. *Why* are we interested in Victorian architecture? *Why* does Victorian architecture – an extraordinary phenomenon anyway – exist at all? In an attempt to answer these two questions I have written this book.

The first question – Why are we interested in Victorian architecture? – is the easier of the two, even if the answer involves a further problem – Why do fashions in taste move forward in time? It was not, after all, until the old Regent Street was demolished in 1928 that the Regency was 'discovered'; and not until television had brought Mr Betjeman's poems to a mass audience – years after they were written – that ordinary people became aware, rather suddenly, that every day they walked in Victorian streets. Somehow or other of course – with or without Mr Betjeman – Victorian architecture would, like that of the Regency, have been rediscovered. William Morris's Society for the Protection of Ancient Buildings, founded in 1878, hardly ventured to protect anything as 'late' as the eighteenth century; for W.S. Gilbert 'art stopped short at the cultivated court of the Empress Josephine'. Then, a generation ago, we had the Georgian Group, and now the Victorian Society. The neo-Georgians will soon be upon us!

But that always happens – first to forget and then to rediscover – with much misunderstanding – the art of one's grandparents. The Victorians themselves, for instance, idealized Georgian England, although they got almost everything wrong. Since they were romantic, industrial and liberal, in self-defence they had to repudiate an era that had been classic, agricultural and aristocratic, to repudiate Georgian elegance, and to discover and idealize other, and often purely imaginary, values.

In a hundred Victorian novels and paintings the Georgian world was idealized, romanticized, sentimentalized ... but of course it was not the Georgian world at all. It was a Victorian dream. The filth, cruelty, crime, stench and snobbery of the eighteenth century were forgotten. Together with the elegance – which really was a Georgian asset – they were replaced by a foolish picture of periwigs, snowclad Christmases, spanking coaches, benevolent squires, highwaymen, Trafalgar, Waterloo and old gabled streets. That the powdered wigs had usually been lice-ridden and their wearers pox-ridden, that the *Victory* had several whores on board, that the troops at Waterloo were the scum of the earth, that Dick Turpin was a nasty sadist, that it seldom snowed at Christmas – twice in Dickens's lifetime – and that the gabled streets were not Georgian at all, were among the things the Victorians chose *not* to know. That Georgian houses were beautiful – the one thing in the dream that might have been true – was ignored. Dickens could dismiss Bath, with all its Augustan beauty, as 'an old rookery'. But then Dickens was an inveterate Victorian: his picture of times present – gaols, workhouses, schools – was devastating; his picture of times past was beneath contempt.

This too, then, would seem to be a law: that each age in repudiating its forerunner, both idealizes and distorts. We are no better. In reversing Victorian values, and idealizing the Victorian world, we have distorted the picture – have done to the Victorians what they once did to the Georgians. The Victorians lived in a world of Georgian towns and villages, and thought it merely dull. So with us: the whole backcloth of our lives – rural and urban – is still mainly Victorian. Most of us, however, see only those bits and pieces – the little old shopfront or the country rectory – which live up to our picture of 'the good old days'. Significantly a much favoured author in air-raid shelters was Trollope; whereas, in fact, Victorian *realpolitik* had paved the way for the bombs.

Nevertheless, for all the bugs, beetles and drains, that quiet world of Barchester or Cranford, that earnest world of Tractarian parsons and Oxford common-rooms, that world of Hardy's peasants buried deep in English shires, did really exist. Of course it did. But it was not very important. By and large Victorian England was a tremendously virile and very terrible affair. If we strip away the gadgets and fashions, Victorian England was not unlike the United States today. There was the same unblinking worship of independence and of hard cash; there was the same belief in institutions – patriotism, democracy, individualism, organized religion, philanthropy, sexual morality, the family, capitalism and Progress; the same excitement and movement; the same overwhelming self-confidence, with its concomitant – a novel and adventurous architecture. And, at the core, was the same tiny abscess – the nagging guilt as to the inherent contradiction between the morality and the system.

For anyone who wishes to study the Victorian Age it was, like our own, complicated but very rich in records. Whether in prose or verse, painting or architecture, or even photography, the Victorians have left us a most detailed picture of themselves. In all spheres of life Mr G. M. Young's *Early Victorian England* (1934) was able to give us one of the most complete pictures of a past epoch that one could wish for. For all that we still go on picking out the pieces of the jig-saw that suit us. The lady of today – dreaming of some age of lavender-scented charm – hangs up a sampler. She forgets the little girl, sore-eyed and constipated, stitching beneath the hard correction of the rod. That lady sets her waxed fruit, her Berlin woolwork, her Victoriana, as splashes of colour against the white wall of her cottage parlour. She forgets the crowded, darkened suburban drawing-room where these things were born, forgets the creatures who dusted them so long ago.

And if in these pages I try to evoke just a little of the vigour, the self-assurance, the sheer artistry of, say, Waterhouse's High Victorian architecture in Manchester, we must never forget that the main contribution of the Victorian Age to architecture is the Slum. If the Town Hall in Manchester is really rather superb, there was also ... the rest of Manchester.

In our admiration and wonder at the grand skyline – the towers of South Kensington or the pinnacles of Whitehall Court – we must remember the other side of the medal. There were the slums; there were also the vast Saharas of suburban roads, commonplace, speculative or merely squalid – occasionally pretentious. We can still take a bus ride – north, south, east or west – from the middle of London, out through all the villages that London has devoured, out and out until we come to the end, to the commuters' housing estates of our own time.

The Londoner of today – despite our own building energy – still lives in a place mainly Victorian. At the core are the two medieval cities, each set in the tangle of medieval lanes that still surround the Abbey and St Paul's. Then, beyond that – the next ring round the heart of the tree trunk – is just a little of the elegant order of the Georgian era, the squares of Bloomsbury or Mayfair. All along the rim of this Georgian London – and the stile at the top of Portland Place was the end of the Town – they built the iron-roofed railway stations. Beyond that, out to Barnet or Epping Forest in the north, to Kingston in the south, to Blackheath in the east, and to Staines or even Windsor in the west – with here and there an oasis of some old village green or common – was Chaos and Old Night.

In that impenetrable forest of houses, railways and canal cuttings, cemeteries, gasworks and gas lamps, Victorian man was bred, and gave birth to our own grandparents. The empire-builders, the little bank clerks, the gin-sodden navvies, the respectable wife-murderers, the pious matrons, the bohemian rebels ... in that great compost of bricks and mortar they built for themselves an architecture ... of sorts.

The architecture of the Victorian Age tells us more about the men who made it than does any other architecture in history. It made such very definite statements about life; it was all so self-assured and vulgar, that it never leaves us in doubt. It never diluted itself – as has our architecture – with inhibitions about style or taste. The Victorian architect knew what he wanted to do and, good or bad, he did it.

Victorian architecture fascinates us, but we must beware. We see it today either as a complete whole, or else surrounded by buildings of our own time. We also see much of it with a hundred years of grime on it. In fact it was a kind of kaleidoscope – as much being demolished as was built – and always against the backcloth of an earlier time. It has been remarked, and Canaletto painted it for us, that Inigo Jones's Banqueting House in Whitehall was once uncompromisingly modern. It out-topped the little brick and timber houses of medieval West-minster. We see it now as an item in a modern street; the seventeenth century saw it as aggressively high and large, white against a clean sky. So we must try to see Victorian architecture. When the Queen went to the Abbey to be crowned, the new Houses of Parliament, just across the road, were hardly begun; Carlton House Terrace was gleam-ing white, and very few of the public offices in Whitehall existed. When the Queen died sixty-four years later, the Imperial Institute was all silver laced with gold, and the town was all round it. Holborn Bars is now a medieval relic for tourists; there was much of that kind of thing, unregarded, in the London of Barry and Butterfield. And the villages all around – Chelsea, Kensington, Battersea, Hampstead and the rest – were still only villages. Farther afield, if the great engines in Sheffield or Birmingham had begun to turn, it was still the cattle markets and the big sailing barges on the Trent or the Ouse that mattered most.

'When the cathedrals were white' is a phrase of Le Corbusier's. Those Victorian hotels, stations and town-halls and museums were once also white and red and raw. With coal fires burning in every room the soot soon fell, but even so there must have been times when the huge Gothic Revival piles reared themselves garishly into the sky while, quite near, were cottages and fields. We think we know what the St Pancras Hotel is like – and that is startling enough. To see it brand new, with the cattle and the hay wains, as well as the cabs, in the muddy, foggy road outside, needs a more conscious effort of the imagination.

There is not much difficulty, therefore, in finding an answer to my first question: why are we interested in Victorian architecture? Being so unlike any other architecture that there ever was, it is fascinating in itself. It is far enough from us to belong to a world utterly unlike our own. It is near enough to us to be all round us every day, and also to be, as it were, the womb from which we have come.

My other question – why did Victorian architecture exist at all? – is more difficult to answer. Of course a virile nation, with a rising population, had to build somehow and somewhere, but why in that particular form – alternately so beautiful and so grotesque? The answer is complex. I hope that this book – rather than adding further to those invaluable lists of names and dates – will give the reader at least a tentative answer.

R. Furneaux Jordan

Ross Bar, Co. Cork, 1964
University of Syracuse, N.Y., 1964–5
Burcombe, Wiltshire, 1965

Acknowledgements

The publishers and author would particularly like to express their gratitude to Miss Caldicott and Miss Morrison of the Architectural Association for their help with certain of the illustrations for this book.

Permission to reproduce other illustrations has been given by the following: Aerofilms Ltd, 4, 14, 75, 87; Aero Pictorial Ltd, 127; T. & R. Annan & Sons Ltd, 45, 79, 107–110; Architectural Association, 10, 117; British Railways (Western Region), 6; *The Builder*, 35, 67; Cadbury Bros Ltd, 130; Central Press Photos, 12; G.L.C., 86; Gordon Charatan, page 22; Chicago Architectural Photographing Company, 136–9; Christie's, 94; *Country Life*, 17, 18, 27, 28, 30, 43, 44, 95, 97–9, 104, 118, 119, 121, 122, 128; Eric de Mare, 2, 3, 7–9, 11, 54, 56, 57, 63, 68, 71, 72, 93, 103, 116, 132; E. R. Jarrett, 77, 78, 89; A. F. Kersting, 5, 19, 32, 38; *Leicester Mercury*, 102; Leicester Museums and Art Gallery, 52; Manchester C.C., 84; Museum of British Transport, 58, 66; National Building Record, 1, 15, 16, 21, 24, 25, 29, 31, 33, 34, 36, 37, 39–42, 46, 49–51, 60, 64, 81, 82, 85, 90, 92, 123–6, 129, 131; George Outram & Co. Ltd, 83; Prestel Verlag, 133; Radio Times Hulton Picture Library, 55, 70, 112; Royal Holloway College, 115; Walter Scott, 120; Scottish National Buildings Record, 114; Edwin Smith, 47, 53, 69, 73; Tate Gallery, 13; Thomas Photos, 48; Victoria and Albert Museum, 65, 88, 96, 111; Walkers Studios Ltd, 80.

Victorian Architecture

T.E.Knightley: Birkbeck Bank

1

The Nature of an Industrial Revolution

Man, by his unique nature – his ability to calculate, stand upright, use his arms and put his thumb over his palm to hold a tool – is an industrial animal. The story of inventions through eight thousand years is virtually a prolonged industrial revolution. But there have been moments when that graph of invention rose to a peak. Such peaks are the *true* industrial revolutions. Life is then permanently changed.

There have, in recent centuries, been three such moments of mounting complexity ... when the brain and the hand collaborate. That collaboration was once technically very simple – carving or painting. We now call it 'science and industry'. Science is what you know, art or industry is what you do – the brain and the hand.

Those three moments have been described by Patrick Geddes (*Cities in Evolution*, 1915) and by Lewis Mumford (*Technics and Civilisation*, 1934). They used terms analogous to those of the geologist; they are precise and have no synonyms. These are the three epochs.

1. The *Eotechnic* (*c.* 1660): wind and water as prime movers; wood as a basic material; merchants as controllers; windmills, wagons and galleons as tools; typical power unit – a turret windmill of 14 h.p.
2. The *Paleotechnic* (*c.* 1860): coal and steam as prime movers; iron as a basic material; *laissez-faire* capitalists as controllers; mobile and static steam engines as tools; typical power unit – Newcomen steam engine of 75 h.p.
3. The *Neotechnic* (*c.* 1960): electricity as prime mover; specialized alloys as basic material; governments as controllers; turbines and computers as tools; typical power unit – a turbo-generator of 75,000 h.p.

We are now moving from the second epoch to the third. For reasons partly historical, mainly geographical, the Low Countries dominated the eotechnical era; England and the Middle West the paleotechnical; while the neotechnical may well be planetary. As each era impinges upon the next it has its appropriate wars and appropriate architecture. The windmill and canal landscape, with the Hanseatic ports, is the corpse of the first era; the railways and the 'black' cities is the corpse of the second; while the arterial roads and dispersed industry will be the corpse of the third.

The Industrial Revolution was not, therefore, a purely Victorian phenomenon – chance product of a few inventions. It was one chapter of a continuous historical process. That process began in medieval England when some man sold cloth instead of wearing a fleece. It is a process still going on ... possibly now out of control.

Each of those three epochs – eotechnic, paleotechnic and neotechnic – had its birth pangs, its moment of high achievement – cities and architecture – and then of slow death or, rather, of slow transmutation into the next epoch. The Victorian Age was nothing more nor less than the achievement period of our second or paleotechnic epoch.

The achievement period of the first or eotechnic epoch arose when the Economic Nationalism of the sixteenth-century Renaissance gave us an Atlantic world as opposed to a Mediterranean one. Bristol, Plymouth, Amsterdam, Antwerp, Cadiz, Boston and Rio replaced Genoa, Alexandria and Venice as the great ports of commerce. It was in Elizabeth's time that in population London first passed Venice. Feudal lords could neither establish nor control economic empires, whether of the New World or the Indies. It was the compass, as much as theological doubt, that spelt the doom of Feudal Christendom.

It was the Atlantic seaboard states, therefore, that were first organized under the absolute monarchies – Hapsburgs, Tudors, Bourbons, all replete with armies, fleets and banks – while Italy and the Germanies had to await the nineteenth century, with its Garibaldis and its Bismarcks, before they could federate.

The so-called wars of religion of the sixteenth and seventeenth centuries were at least as economic as they were religious. The wealth of the Spanish Main, as well as the nature of a sacrament, were at stake when the Armada set sail. And out of the English Civil War, two generations later, there was born ultimately, not Puritanism but a new governing class – designed to stop the diversion of profits to a dying courtier class through the granting of monopolies. Two centuries later, in Victorian England, that same governing class were themselves demanding 'royalties' wherever their parks or farms lay above the coal.

That eotechnic epoch, with its canals and mills at home, its galleons overseas, needed its markets and empires no less than the nineteenth century. Spain disposed of, it was the Flemish and English merchants – Antwerp and the City – who dominated the achievement period of the eotechnic epoch, as Manchester and Chicago dominated the paleotechnic and – incidentally – gave us Waterhouse and Lloyd Wright.

The cause of wars, in the last analysis, is that regions of economic power and regions of political control, seldom coincide. Prehistoric men went to war when the pasture or the fishing ground was in dispute. The eotechnic merchants needed the Americas, the Barbary Coast, or the Isles of Spice before they could build their fine town houses and noble quays, before they could build, say, Longleat or the streets of Haarlem. Equally the Manchester merchants, before they could build Waterhouse's town-hall or the Ship Canal, or the Ruskinian villas of Didsbury, needed the cotton fields of the Deep South. Whether through alliance or direct control, the gentlemen of Virginia and the Indian princes were both necessary to Lancashire mills. Given that link then the stage was set for the 'Workshop of the World', for the emergence of the paleotechnic from the eotechnic. Such things, as well as factories and engines, are part of the nature of an industrial revolution, and for such things are architectures built.

Industrialism is a cooperative process. Every invention depends upon others. The motor-car, for instance, involves not only the exploitation of two fuels, petrol and electricity – the explosive gas and the igniter – but also a host of other inventions such as the means to bore cylinders, to make pneumatic tyres and macadam roads. It then creates, whether in Coventry, Dagenham or Cowley, an affluent proletariat, an affluent consumer.

Iron was cast, instead of wrought, in the year 1400. It was neither plentiful nor useful until the invention of coke-smelting by Abraham Darby about 1717. The Coalbrookdale Bridge, in Shropshire, wholly

1 Abraham Darby: Coalbrookdale Bridge

of iron and spanning 100 feet, was finished in 1779 [1]. After that the British production of pig-iron rose from 62,000 tons in 1788 to a quarter of a million by 1806. In 1828 came the invention of Neilson's hot-blast; thereafter production grew to three million tons by the middle of the century, to eight million by the end. The basic material of the paleotechnic epoch was established. Without that material neither the looms nor the lathes, neither the mills nor the mines, neither the trains nor the rails, neither the steamers nor the docks would have been possible.

Finally, through the Bessemer process, iron could be transformed into steel. Before the steel could be a skyscraper you had to invent the lift, pile-driving, cranes and high-level plumbing. Then, but only then, Manhattan and Chicago were also possible.

If iron was the basic material of the Victorian Age, its prime mover was coal ... or coal's derivative, steam. Even in the eotechnic epoch, between 1550 and 1680, the annual production of coal – without mechanical cutting – had risen from less than a quarter of a million tons to nearly three million. The industrial security of Victorian England, however, hung – so it was said – upon the picks of barely two hundred thousand miners. At the Queen's accession there were still more cobblers than miners in England, and more domestic servants in London alone. The miners' wages by mid-century, were 3s. to 4s. a day. As the long tentacles of the railways spread, their numbers and their wages rose. Moreover, like the railway navvies, they were reinforced by Irish labour. In 1847, after the great potato famine, three hundred thousand Irish landed in Liverpool alone; there they might sleep forty in a basement room until – tramping the roads or riding on the penny-a-mile Parliamentary trains – they could disperse to the coalfields and the mills. The nature of an industrial revolution – at its moment of achievement – is that of a Gold Rush. In Victorian England that is disguised because it is all set against an older society and an older landscape ... but the high and greedy optimism and the same frenetic desperation were all there.

The coal came first mainly from Northumberland and Durham; then the Black Country was created by the chance that coal and a fine casting sand lay side by side. By the forties the valleys of South Wales all running down to the boom cities of Swansea, Cardiff and Newport, were mined. The Welsh coal was needed for the locomotives of Brunel's Great Western which, by 1848, was doing the Paddington–Didcot run at 57 m.p.h. But that coal was also part of an international traffic. Just as Manchester's raw cotton was coming from Virginia to go out again – as white robes for the teeming millions of the Ganges Valley – so the Bryn Mawr or Merthyr Tydfil coal went out from Swansea to Chile, whence the same iron-plated ships brought back copper.

So, the industrial revolution was social, technical, geographical and, perhaps above all, geological. The geological map of England is a tidy one; those broad bands of chalk and oolite and clay and fen run clearly across the land from south-west to north-east leaving the west for the granite highlands of Scotland and Wales. Interspersed in that clear pattern are the grey patches of the coal measures – Lanark, Tyneside, Lancashire, Yorkshire, the Black Country and South Wales.

Each geological area has been the scene, the focus, at some time or

2 Stockport Viaduct and Canal

other, of some architecture. When the chalk once lay bare and grassy above the choked rivers and forests, primitive man could there cultivate the slopes and make his trackways, and there, in Stonehenge, leave us his monument. In the Middle Ages the sheep and wool of the downs and of the oolitic or limestone belt, which embraces the Cotswolds, was the basis of the English cloth trade. That cloth was sent all across Europe and, by happy chance, those sheeplands overlay the finest freestone in the world. The wealth and well-being of Medieval and Tudor England – with its churches, cottages and manors – was concentrated upon the oolite. If, centuries later, Brunel's locomotives were served by the Welsh coal valleys, his railway served the great country houses of the West of England.

The eotechnical epoch – the industrial revolution of wood and wind – was concentrated upon the newly drained fens and fertile East Anglian flats, while the big, slow, smug rivers, like the Trent and the Ouse, were busy with sailing barges.

3 Jesse Hartley: Albert Docks, Liverpool

Victorian England was yet one more shift in the geological pattern – sure sign that it really was a new technical epoch and not merely the story of a few inventions – an industrial revolution being social as well as mechanical, also geological. It was a shift from the oolite, the lias and the sand to the coal measures. What had been the wooded hills of Yorkshire or Wales became, almost overnight, a land of squalid villages and black, roaring, crowded cities [2]. Villages and small country markets became the Birminghams and Glasgows that we know. The railways and factories needed the coal, and the railways linked the factories to the new ports ... the model of the Liverpool Docks was the showpiece of the Great Exhibition of 1851 [3].

Agriculture disperses, coal concentrates, then electricity again disperses. The men, women and children of the older agricultural England – ten million or so – had been thinly spread over the land. Coal and steam meant the concentration of labour in factories, of factories around the pits or in towns where the main lines could bring them

4 Tower Bridge. *Coming near the end of the century, this set-piece of the tourist's London is a rare instance of where – owing to the proximity of the Tower – a conscious effort was made to combine a rather heavy 'in-keeping-with' Gothic, with the ingenious mechanics of the elevated bridge.*

5 Addison Road, Kensington. *If some of the later Georgian architects – Nash among them – were glorified spec' builders, by the forties there were spec' builders who could turn out a stucco facade in whatever mode was in demand – classic or, as here, Gothic.*

coal. Then, in our time, electricity once again dispersed the people – fifty million or so – to the suburban sprawl, the new towns and the light industries of the south-east. It was the sheer geological concentrations of the Victorian paleotechnic that produced the towns, slums and architecture of the nineteenth century. Those big Victorian cities may have been mainly slums and factories but, because of their sheer size, they needed the churches, banks and big town-halls. They were the first prerequisite of a Victorian architecture.

In the census of 1851 the agricultural population – still thought of as 'the great central productive class' – employed just over two million, but industry and commerce now employed five-and-a-half million. By 1865 a quarter of the population lived in cities of 100,000 or more. There had been five such cities in England – London apart – in 1831. By 1861 there were eleven. By 1900 half the people lived in five cities. The population when Queen Anne died was eight million; when Victoria died thirty million; it is now fifty million.

London, even before the railways came, had been growing by a quarter of a million every ten years. The railways doubled that rate of growth. It was not, however, until the middle of the century that London actually began to spread, that the City ceased to be the place where the bankers and the bank clerks actually lived. The Metropolitan Railway – the 'underground' – opened in 1863, and there was thus born one of the biggest single facts in the story of Victorian architecture – the suburb.

The same sort of story could be told of Manchester, Liverpool, Birmingham, Leeds, Sheffield, Bradford and Glasgow. Their suburbs might be slums; or they might – like Didsbury, Sefton Park, Edgbaston or Headingley – be an estate of 'desirable villas in their own grounds' possessing sometimes a charming, if belated, hangover from the Regency.

In the main, however, urban growth was a tale of squalor, cruelty and death. In 1860 the son of a gentleman in Bath could expect fifty-five years of life; the son of a labourer in Liverpool fifteen years. As the nineteenth century ran its course life on the whole got a little safer ... for some. By 1830 the infant mortality rate for the upper class had been reduced to one in ten; for the lower class it had risen to one in four. One cause of mass decimation was cholera – the 'Asiatic Cholera' which ravaged town after town and was hardly mitigated, as in Exeter, by the public but charitable issue of flannel belts. The real cure came slowly. It came only when the money was found for sewers. The communal privies, the open kennels, the cesspools leaking into wells and beneath the floors of crowded rooms, had been the cause. Thus through the upper-class fear that cholera might spread, the basis of the modern city came into being. Without water-borne sewage neither London nor New York could exist.

In the eighteenth century there were mills everywhere – whether wind or water. Some, such as the famous ones along the Stroud Valley in Gloucestershire, were virtually water-power factories, with several hundred 'hands', iron shafting and iron columns to support the floors. There were forges that were also factories, at least compared with the village blacksmiths. All through the eighteenth century the technical invention graph climbed steadily, but significantly it is concerned mainly either with agriculture – seed drills and even, in 1786, a thresher – or with the mechanization of domestic crafts. There had, it is true, been a trip-forge hammer in 1320, a screw-cutting lathe in 1550, a knitting machine in 1589, a ribbon loom in 1621 and so on ... but how slow the tempo. Moreover life itself was untouched.

Then, quite suddenly, everything quickens. Although the list is still mainly one of looms, shuttles, carding machines and cotton printing, life was being changed a little all the time. England remained agricultural and rural, but the long era of cottage industry was ending. Kay's flying-shuttle came in 1733, cotton printing in 1783. These, with the famous Spinning Jenny of 1768 and the Cotton Gin of a few years later were – ultimately – to make possible the great Gothic Revival buildings of Victorian Manchester. They were the technical basis for a wealth of which the political basis already existed, waiting only to be secured and sealed with the enfranchisement of the bosses in the Reform Bill of 1832.

As the eighteenth century moves to its close the wheels are already turning in some of the great tools of heavy industry – the Newcomen engines, Crompton's mule and Watt's rotative steam engine, all in the eighties. After that they come thick and fast. The 'Gold Rush' is on. The new century opens with Trevithick's rail engine. Fulton's S.S. *Clermont* and Stephenson's first locomotive came in the year before Waterloo, centrifugal pumps, a calculating machine and an attempt at an internal combustion engine follow. Steam road-carriages, the first embryonic electric generator and the 'Rocket's' run from Stockton to Darlington heralded by a few years the Queen's accession.

After that the deluge. Turbines and propellors (1836), drop-forging and die-stamping (1835), the telegraph (1837), compressed air and disc-cutting in coal mines (1852), the start of effective alloys and aluminium in 1855 and Bessemer's steel a year later. Gas-turbines, machine-guns, winding gear, open-hearth steel and the typewriter belong to the sixties. Chain coal-cutters, a refrigerator, a petrol engine, a combine harvester, the telephone and Benz's motor-car belong to the seventies, while incandescent lamps, public electric lighting, heavy oil engines, welding, the gramophone, the Dunlop tyre and the tractor belong to the eighties. If the conveyor belt and the assembly line seem to belong only to the automobile factory of our own time, they were in fact being used almost a century earlier for pig carcasses in the Chicago meat factories.

Meanwhile those tough, ingenious self-made men who 'navigated' the railways were wearing themselves out – days in the saddle, nights in carriages, an early death. Stephenson, Brunel [6], and Locke all died in their fifties. When *Pickwick* was published in 1836 there were railway projects in the air, but the old coach roads were untouched. The mails still set off from St Martin-le-Grand – as they had done with garlands around them after Trafalgar – and the ritual of changing horses still went on at every posting house. By 1848 – the boom year –

when *Dombey and Son* could tell of 'the fiery devil ... with its lurid smoke', there were over five thousand miles of railway line in England, two thousand under construction by nearly a quarter of a million navvies. The Great North Road had become a parish highway, while the Holyhead Road, newly built by Telford to get the Dublin Mails through by 'flyer', was already grass-grown – waiting for the motor-car a hundred years hence.

The popular supposition that an industrial revolution, by means of a new technique such as cast-iron, changes architectural style is an inadequate thesis. By changing life and thought it also changes radically the whole function and aesthetic of architecture.

Perhaps the greatest single industrial or technical revolution in history came about when the Roman engineers first understood and

6 Isambard Kingdom Brunel

7 I.K.Brunel: Royal Albert Bridge, Saltash

8 Warehouses, Manchester

9 Thomas Telford: St Katherine's Dock, London

exploited the arch and its derivatives – vaults and domes. From that flowed all the styles of two thousand years – Roman, Byzantine, Romanesque, Gothic and Baroque. That is true. It is only part of the story. The materialistic and practical Roman mind made of the Roman not only an engineer but an administrator and empire-builder. From that there followed not only vaults and domes but all the innumerable types of building needed in a great cosmopolitan capital, as well as all the cities of the provinces from Scotland to Jerusalem. And upon the foundations of those cities, and the roads linking them together, our world came into being.

The Victorian Age is a parallel situation. The exploitation of iron and glass – and many other innovations – would, in any case, have produced a new architecture. That was obvious by the middle of the eighteenth century – with its iron bridges [7] and its plain, strong warehouses belonging to what J.M. Richards has called 'the Functional Tradition' [8, 9]. Far more pregnant for architecture, however, than any structural change, was the concentration of population within big cities, and the railways linking them.

The rise of the big cities changed thought. The true significance of the Industrial Revolution did not lie in technical changes – great as these were – but in intellectual and spiritual ones.

With the shift from an agricultural to an industrial England, an old and well-defined society vanished. On the one hand there had been the gentry – nobility, squirearchy and professions; on the other there had been the peasantry. (Symbolically the Reform Act of 1832 marks the passing of the former, the Education Act of 1870 the passing of the latter.) The gentry had for too long been the patrons of a 'polite' and elegant classicism – the very insignia of their status being the Adam fireplace or Georgian doorway; while the peasantry had been the patrons of the pedlar, of the ancient crafts and of those immemorial ways of building that we call the vernacular.

In an industrial England the gentry must have seemed – as in Ireland today – to be living in a half-forgotten backwater of country houses and decaying parks. They still had their rent rolls; they were not yet impoverished nor had their titles lost all their magic; they merely did not count. Their place had been taken by a wholly new and wholly urban class of master and magnate. Not all these were the

10 Carriages in Hyde Park

nouveaux-riches bosses of legend; many were hypocritical or ruthless – in a cut-throat world – but many were also enlightened, cultured and pious, not least those Quakers, Unitarians and agnostics who, being much concerned with the condition of the people – 'the deserving poor' – were also the backbone of model municipalities. Liverpool, Manchester, Birmingham – for all their horrors and wealth – were among the best governed cities in the world. The foundations were being laid for that kind of local government now responsible for almost all our housing and almost all our schools. These 'new men' of the cities were not all boors. If they had never learnt to turn a Latin hexameter at Eton, they could love their Scott, their Ruskin, Tennyson or Browning ... also the sights of Venice and of Florence. Culture and enlightenment, as they saw it, meant not – as it had so often done – the unread, calf-bound volumes of a country-house library; it meant art schools, concert halls, public libraries and institutes, church schools, gaols [11], workhouses, orphanages and, above all, new churches. These – as well as the two poles of slums and prosperous suburbs – were the architectural core of the nineteenth-century city.

Watts's steam kettle may have led directly to railways and to great iron railway stations; more indirectly it led to the whole wealth and population, and therefore to the whole architecture, of the Victorian Age. The nature of an industrial revolution is such that its consequences are immeasurable.

2

The Nature of a Romantic Movement

The Romantic Movement – like the Renaissance – was an upheaval in the long continuity of European culture. Victorian architecture, painting and music were a late phase of that movement.

Romanticism is the Divine Discontent of the artist – his flight from the cruel reality of the present into a dream world, into a world that is strange or distant, whether in time or space. For thousands of years the artist, whether as the anonymous craftsman of a universal culture such as that of Attica or of the Middle Ages, or as the professional in an aristocratic culture such as the Roman or the Baroque, had been acceptable to society. Always, in some craft or other, he had been on the band-wagon of his time. He had been taken for granted as is the skilled technician today. Only towards the end of the eighteenth century and, even more, in the nineteenth century, did the artist suddenly discover himself to be a Bohemian, a rebel against all social norms – in short, a Romantic. Nothing has ever been the same since.

Romanticism, therefore, implies revolt. The particular power and universality of the Romantic Movement lay in its revolt against both tradition and progress, against both classicism and industrialism. It is regarded primarily as a cultural movement, whereas its first manifestation was the French Revolution, its last the Russian one. It changed the world.

In the eighteenth century the romantic was in revolt merely against the conventions, fashions and tyrannies of an aristocratic régime. The Age of Reason had become so reasonable as to be ineffably boring; the social system so unjust as to be unbearable; classical art so systematized as to be meaningless. One consequence among many – a trivial one – was the English eccentrics such as the Walpoles or Beckfords toying with their Gothic follies and sham castles. Another consequence was all that earnest piety and enthusiasm that gave birth in due course to so many Gothic churches.

In the nineteenth century the romantic although still, as always, a rebel against aristocracy and academic traditions, was, far more, a rebel against the cruelty, squalor and ugliness of the whole urban and industrial system. He could either flee to his dreams – that dream world of an idealized past or an idealized Nature; or he could protest. In the event he did both. Romanticism in one way or another thus penetrated almost every sphere.

Romanticism was only one facet of that complicated thing we call the Victorian Age. There was also and above everything: industry, business, society, convention, class, the Constitution and Money. There was also Domesticity – those new-found domestic virtues designed to offset Regency looseness – and their corollary, Sentiment. One can, for instance, think of Queen Victoria's drawing-room at

12 Queen Victoria's drawing-room, Osborne House

Windsor or Osborne House, crammed with a thousand carefully labelled knick-knacks, there not because of their intrinsic merits, but solely because of association or sentiment. The locket Albert gave her at Coburg, the children photographed on ponies at Laeken; the shells they collected, the woolwork by an old nurse, the statuette of John Brown ... then one recalls that, after all, the Queen's own rooms were only a reflection of other prosperous drawing-rooms or even, surburban parlours. Sentimentality is really, however, only a kind of romanticism. It is an escape to dreams, but it is romanticism without the artist. It was one of the strongest forces of the Victorian Age – second only to Money. All the same, in the end and as always, it was the artist, not Sentiment or Money, who changed the Victorian scene, who changed every artifact. The world one looked upon in 1800 and the world one looked upon in 1900 were two different worlds.

In his *Decline and Fall of the Romantic Ideal* (1936), F. L. Lucas quotes these two verses from Heine:

> On a bare northern hillside,
> A lonely fir-tree grows,
> Nodding in its white mantle
> Of ice and driven snows.

> And of a palm its dream is,
> That sorrows, mute, alone,
> In some far land of morning,
> On hills of burning stone.

Now to some calm cynic of the Augustan Age these verses would appear ludicrous – one tree dreaming of another! In fact, with their sensitivity and yearning melancholy, they are one of Heine's more memorable laurels. They symbolize the eternal yearning of the North for the South, of the artist for that dream world, for that Holy Grail he will never find. When we add to them Heine's own definition of Romanticism: 'a reawakening of the Middle Ages ... a passion flower blooming from the blood of Christ', we have assembled most of the elements of a Romantic Movement – chivalry, love, religion, strangeness and sadness.

A Romantic Movement, then, is the divine discontent of the artist. If, very often, it is just a withdrawal to ivory towers, it is also rebellion against both the boredoms of a cold and conventional classicism, and against THE SYSTEM.

That divine discontent of the artist is escape to the strange and distant, to the Indies, to Xanadu, to Iceland, to the Hebrides – 'and we in dreams behold the Hebrides' – or to the Middle Ages, to Fairylands forlorn, to candles on dim altars, to blue distances, over the hills and far away; or perhaps to low life, whether to the cottage of Morland's peasants or to Borrow's gypsy camp; to sad ruins by moonlight, to delicious decay, to *The Haystack in the Floods*, to Andrew Keith of Ravelstone riding down the glen, to Beata Beatrix or *The White Doe of Rylstone*. One sees knights journeying forever through the neat orchards and cornlands of the illuminated missal, past little whitewalled towns or by broad rivers, riding towards Camelot; or shepherds wandering from one grey monastery to another, half lost in the bog or oak forests of Ireland. Or there is a mullioned, lichened house, half manor, half farm, set by its own smooth mill pond; it is called Lone End, Kelmscott or the Moated Grange – or anything you wish; we see a swan gliding quietly from the shadows with a golden collar round her neck. It is not the Cotswolds; it is the Cotswolds of our dreams, or it is the fairy meres of Connemara. It is all the stuff of dreams made real in concrete images. It is also in effect the transference of the Grand Tour from Imperial Rome to the Gothic North or to the Celtic twilight.

That is the Victorian vision. In poetry it is everything from Coleridge to Yeats, in painting from Turner and the Pre-Raphaelites to the Impressionists, and in architecture from Beckford's sham abbey at Fonthill on to Le Corbusier's pilgrim church at Ronchamp.

That vision may seem sometimes to have been hopelessly lost in the stark reality of Victorian bricks and mortar; all the same it was the mainspring of Victorian art. In our context, that vision was the passionate inspiration of the Gothic Revival, the seed from which eventually there sprang a hundred ugly parish churches.

Now, to a Dr Johnson, a Pope, a Gibbon, a Lord Chesterfield, to Squire Weston or Parson Woodeford, all this romanticism would have seemed a pack of nonsense. To them a sprightly fancy was permissible, but all this – with a hint even of opium or chloral in the background – would have seemed delirium. Yet a generation later, with the Romantic poets, it was the very stuff of our culture and, with the St Martin's Summer of Pre-Raphaelitism and the Gothic Revival, remained so for over a century. If we are to understand the architecture of the Victorian Age we must ask why.

The half century between 1790 and 1840 is unique in our history for the number of great men – sensitive, imaginative, perceptive, creative – born in this island. The list is a long one. It must, at the very least, include Turner, Constable, Girtin, Walter Scott, Samuel Palmer, Blake, Shelley, Keats, Coleridge, Wordsworth, Byron, Charlotte Yonge, Pugin, Butterfield, Gilbert Scott, Pater, Christina Rossetti, the six Pre-Raphaelites, Ruskin, Morris, Newman, Keble, Carlyle, Emily Brontë, the Brownings and Tennyson. Why, it is worth asking, was every one of these giants opposed in some way or other to what we would call 'the Establishment'? Why, it is worth asking, was every one of them concerned in some way or other with this romanticism, this vast unreality, this – to use the modern phrase – unparalleled escapism?

The answer may be brief. First: the life of Georgian England, in all its frigid elegance, had run its course. It had always had limitations more severe than we now admit. We see the terraces of Georgian Bath as they are today, while the Georgian slums and hovels have all gone. For the Victorians, Georgian England – with its splendours and miseries – had become a bore, it had become blousy. Second: scientific inquiry, with all its consequent spiritual doubts, had produced a new earnestness in all religions; no denomination escaped a fervent revival. Third: that same science had created an industrial system to the dire consequences of which the only intelligent response was either retreat ... or battle. Fourth: that same industrialism had created a *bourgeoisie* – educated but not classically educated – philistine and rich, yet hungry for escapism and romanticism. It was in Manchester or Liverpool that Ruskin and Tennyson were read aloud round the lamplit table, and that Pre-Raphaelite pictures were enjoyed. It was in the black cities of the North that the new churches, as well as the town-halls were built.

All those men and women of the Romantic Movement were as varied as were their media, yet we do see that Turner's *Calais Beach* and, say, *Wuthering Heights*; or *The Stones of Venice* and, say, the Houses of Parliament, do have in common with each other something that none of them share with the Royal Crescent at Bath or *The School for Scandal*. That 'something' is almost indefinable: it is the intensity of passion without which a work of art is no more than a seemly arrangement of words or forms. And the Victorian Age, for all its pruderies, was nothing if not passionate. The things it created might often be hideous; they were always deeply felt. The creative imagination, not mere scholarship, was the mainspring of the Victorian Age. That was why it so often failed, so often fell short of its own ideals, was so conscious of its own failure.

As T. S. Eliot has pointed out, between Dr Johnson on the one hand, and Coleridge on the other, lies a great watershed of human thought. For Johnson – or in architecture, say, Chambers or Kent – passion or the romantic imagination were unimportant, even suspect. For the nineteenth century they were fundamental. That the imagination so often – but not always – found its fulfilment in some kind of medievalism may have been inevitable, but was actually incidental. It was the elevation of sensitivity, of the imagination itself that mattered ... the realization of visions and ideals, the creation of dream worlds. The artist in every sphere believed that to deny or curb this faculty of the imagination was a betrayal of self, a betrayal of the Divine Being with whom each shared the creative act. The materialistic philosophy of Locke – the mechanistic universe with man as onlooker – was anathema. The divine and mystical nature of the universe was now discoverable not only in revelation or theology, but even more in Nature and in Man himself. The universe, which science was ever widening and of which Man was part, embraced all things, not least Man's imagination.

This world of Imagination [wrote Blake], is the world of Eternity; it is the bosom into which we shall all go after the death of the vegetated body. This World of the Imagination is Infinite and Eternal, whereas the world of Generation or Vegetation, is Finite and Temporal. . . . All things are comprehended in their Eternal Forms in the divine body of the saviour, the true voice of Eternity, the Human Imagination.

And Coleridge wrote:

The Primary IMAGINATION I hold to be the living Power and prime Agent of all human perception, and as a repetition in the finite mind of the eternal act of creation in the infinite I AM.

When Coleridge wrote that he was saying that imagination is of the first importance because it partakes of the creativity of God. Coleridge would not deny that, as mere man, he could use images and symbols taken only from the finite and concrete world; but in the living corpses and the pale wan stars that hung over the slimy sea of *The Ancient Mariner* he performed a creative act as surely as did ever God. The concrete images – corpses, stars and sea – combine to create overtones more tremendous than themselves, not less tremendous because indefinable. Coleridge felt that the mere act of imagining was itself transcendental; that unearthly powers were at work on earth, that he was entrapping them, making them more vivid than the real world, giving them that sharp dreamlike clarity that was one day to make so real and yet so dreamy almost every Pre-Raphaelite painting, every Morris tapestry, and which – often against tremendous material odds – was attempted by every Gothic Revival architect.

That – the elevation of the Imagination – was the essence, the very starting point of the Romantic Movement. It informed the whole art and architecture of the nineteenth century. However misused or mis-applied, this was the real afflatus of Victorian architecture. Mere form or structure – the first of which had been dominant in the eighteenth century and the second of which was to be dominant in the twentieth century – were altogether subordinate to this passionate embracement of the Imagination.

True, the undisciplined exercise of the Imagination might lead the artist down devious ways. It led to the distortion of architecture by all manner of irrelevancies, theological or liturgical theories, moral or aesthetic convictions. The literary, liturgical or moral, combined, however, to set the second hall-mark upon Victorian romantic art. The first had been this use of the creative imagination; the second was Medievalism – that curious thing running through the whole age, dubbed by Ruskin as 'gothic opinions'.

There was never any intrinsic reason why a romantic art should assume a medieval guise, and in fact it did not always do so. A Romantic Movement, penetrating life at every point, could assume many guises and take upon itself many unexpected forms. It did take many forms; it was in architecture that those forms were mainly medieval. And this was not mere chance.

Some landed aristocrat, standing beneath the portico of his country seat, about the time of the Queen's accession, could still look out on the serene unchanging world of mansion, farm and market. His rent rolls were secure, his taste was correct, his sovereignty undenied. The symbolic clouds on that serene horizon were still faint. There were three such clouds: industrialism, liberalism, romanticism. The last, which was feared least, was to be the real storm [13].

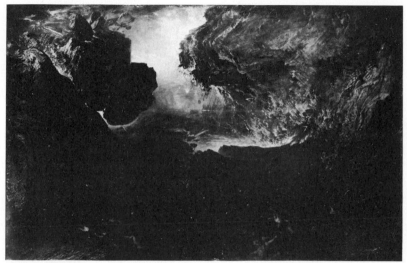

13 John Martin: *The Great Day of His Wrath*

Industrialism, after all, if the factories and railways were kept on the other side of the hill, if the smoke did not drift across those carefully planted glades, could be as profitable for the old aristocrat as for the new magnate ... a few stately homes are still maintained on urban ground rents.

Liberalism, God knows, was serious enough, a menace to property and to religion. The High Tory resented the assumption of power and wealth by the new capitalist ... but, after all, the Reform Bill had been and gone, Radicalism and Chartism were firmly contained within the new towns upon the coal measures. In the great parks and farms of early Victorian England, the world – so it seemed – could go on for-ever.

Romanticism was another story. It struck nearer home. It struck everywhere. It was the beat culture of its day. Not only did it reveal itself in the novels and poetry one read, the pictures one bought and the style of new buildings; it also, astonishingly, changed men's most fundamental thoughts. With its curious ideas about self-help on the one hand, and philanthropy on the other hand, it was even the main-spring of those other two monsters – Industrialism and Liberalism. It was all very disturbing.

Romanticism, being a dual revolt against both the past – classicism and tradition – and against the present – capitalism – was all-pervad-ing and insidious. It was not, however, entirely new. Our Victorian romanticism was the late phase of a much greater movement. Looking back over the previous century we see how one great figure after another – if only as a fashion – had dominated men's minds.

There had for instance been Frederick the Great. Although he seems now to have been the most typical of all Baroque figures – builder of Sans Souci and inventor of the six-foot guardsman – he did in fact, in those endless conversations with Voltaire on such subjects as the nature of Liberty and Justice, flatter himself into believing that he was looking forward just a little towards the romanticism of the next century.

Then there had been Napoleon – so fanatically traditional that he had had to marry a 'daughter of the Caesars' as a kind of status symbol, had had to receive in the opera house at Dresden the homage of all the Baroque monarchs of Europe – and yet, for all that, marched his armies to Moscow under the *tricoleur* of the Revolution. There had been Goethe, and all the *gemütlich* romanticism and charm of gentle Weimar. Strangest of all, in England, there had been Byron and the whole Byronic myth, with all its overtones of license, liberty and swooning love.

Thus, for almost a century, in a world of Baroque or Classical archi-tecture – whether in Paris, Vienna or Bath – the foundations of romantic thinking had been laid. And now, in the Victorian Age, that kind of thinking was everywhere.

There was, for example, Romanticism and Liberty. This meant not only Voltaire and Rousseau, the noble savage, the simple life and the natural man; it meant also that great upsurge of the human spirit – Liberty, Equality, Fraternity ... once Carlyle had pointed it out. It also found its expression in other directions. Before the Victorian era had opened there had, in the Romantic poets, been this passionate love of Liberty. There had been Byron's almost symbolic death at Missolonghi; Wordsworth's dithyrambic hymn to the French Revolution – 'bliss was it in that dawn to be alive' – or Shelley's invective against Peterloo or Castlereagh – 'that smile like a silver plate on a coffin'.

The whole Victorian Age thereafter was not, as we sometimes like to think, an age of placidity, it was one of enthusiastic gestures and high liberal acts. There was the Commune and the Risorgimento abroad, Reform and Chartism at home, the work started by Wilberforce for the Slaves, by Elizabeth Fry in prisons, by Shaftesbury in the slums, by Florence Nightingale in hospitals ... and so on. It was a fervent age.

Such things, it may be said, have little to do with a Romantic Movement, less to do with architecture. In fact they could never have happened if the old aristocratic tradition had not died. They were part and parcel of the artists' protest. All this liberalism was inspired by writers, painters and architects. Dickens's analysis of the workhouse, the slum and low-life generally, Bell Scott's *Iron and Coal*, or Doré's devastating drawings were not only highly romantic – they also attracted that large public whose conscience they pricked. An extraordinary fact about Victorian art, seldom noted, is that its sentiment, realism and anecdotal qualities – all those things that our century has disliked about it – were the very things that made it so wildly popular with the very people – that great, unromantic, philistine middle-class – whom it castigated most. As propaganda, therefore, it has never been equalled. It helped to lay the foundations of the Welfare State a hundred years later.

Romanticism and Nature: if romanticism means escape, then it means escape not only from realms distant in Time or Space, but to realms distant also from life's hard realities – not least an escape to Nature. In any case all those distant realms – golden ages of mythology, lotus isles, Indies, the Middle Ages – always seem to the artist just a little nearer to Nature than does ever the squalid present.

This had always been true. The Greek temple, ideally, had always been seen against a dark-wine Homeric sea; the medieval minster towers across cornfields or above a belt of trees; the Holy Families of the Italian Primitives against the distant vineyards of Tuscany. But this idealization of Nature was of course specially true of a self-consciously romantic epoch, even if it goes back, as it does, rather further in time than do more specifically romantic attitudes to such things as architectural style. It goes back, for instance, to the Elizabethan garden, the *parterre* and the rose plot – as well as to, say, *The Tempest* and all the Sonnets, as well as to those vast 'prodigy houses' of the Loire Valley or of Elizabethan noblemen ... the Renaissance, almost before it was born, romanticizing the medieval castle, almost before the Middle Ages were dead.

If the Elizabethan attitude to Nature was a poetic idealization of a medieval and, indeed, Chaucerian mood, it was also still medieval in that it preferred Nature enclosed, walled and trimmed, abhorring it when it was truly natural or untamed. In the next century – the century of John Evelyn's *Sylva* and of the real planting of the English park and landscape – Man's command over Nature was extended; he now feared it less but still desired the self-assurance and self-flattery of a visible control. This visible control was exemplified most fully in the Baroque, in, say, the radiating avenues of Karlsruhe, the well-drilled formalities of a Schönbrunn or the vast geometry of a Versailles – the quintessence of the Baroque in that it stamped artificial man's artificial pattern upon the landscape, thereby utilizing Nature to deny Nature's existence. The mountain, the ocean and the moor were still beyond the pale.

But that same seventeenth century had also been the century of the landscape painters – of Claude Lorraine, of Nicolas Poussin and of the great Dutchmen. In these landscapes, for convention's sake a few classical figures or even a temple might be introduced – as in Poussin's *Ashes of Phocis* – but it was now the landscape that mattered, not just the landscape as background. Nature, in at least some of its larger forms, could now be looked upon with delight. Thus it was in eighteenth-century England, ultimately, that Lancelot ('Capability') Brown's carefully careless glades and serpentine lakes – the devised pastoral – replaced the great formal avenues and vistas as the setting for the great house. Before that century closed the cult of the 'Picturesque' had been established by Uvedale Price, by Humphrey Repton and by John Nash.

About the cult of the 'Picturesque' there were some things that were ludicrous, there were many that were poetic and charming. The sham Gothic ruin, the shell garden, the grotto with its hermit, and the *cottage ornée* – whether a gabled lodge or a thatched dairy, were among the more foolish things ... although even these must be recognized as a romantic and deliberate gesture against the large and pompous formalities of an earlier generation. Among the better things was the astonishing importation into England of trees and plants – how many new trees belong to those years may be seen at Kew – with all the consequent beauty of rich foliage patterns such as we can see in, say, St James's or Regent's Park, or in the pale greens and dark greens of willows and cedars to be found on the smooth lawns of country seats or in rectory gardens.

14 Buckingham Palace and St James's. *A typically nineteenth-century mess of pottage – the elegance of Nash to the north of the Mall; the heavily restored Palace – built by Nash and Porden and refaced by Aston Webb – and then the big pretentious houses of Hyde Park Corner. England was never good at town-planning in the formal or Grand Manner, and the Mall and Constitution Hill cannot compete with Paris or Vienna or even Washington. In any case Constitution Hill was a Royal and Private Road until this century.*

Even the *cottage ornée*, moreover, if often no more than a garden 'conceit' could become, in the nineteenth century, the estate cottage or the entire estate village. At Blaise, near Bristol, in 1811, John Nash had built a 'model' village of thatched and gabled cottages around a green [15]. If this was a typical manifestation of the 'Picturesque', it was also a forerunner. In 1839, at Edensor, near Chatsworth, Joseph Paxton and John Robertson had built for the Duke of Devonshire another estate village – an odd medley of styles, but also 'commodious and comfortable' – apparently even sanitary. If this, with other such villages, is the precursor of those twentieth-century garden cities of the enlightened industrialist – the Bournvilles and Port Sunlights – it may also be seen as having its genesis in a poetic idealization of Nature (the village in its pastoral setting), also of the Middle Ages (a vernacular architecture revived), and of Low Life (the peasant) ... three well-recognized aspects of Romanticism.

The relevance to Victorian architecture of this changed attitude to Nature was not, however, merely a matter of foliage patterns, of informal gardens, or even of that appreciation of the picturesque which began with pretty cottages and culminated in the New Towns of our own day. As one aspect of the artist's Divine Discontent, it was far more subtle than that, also much deeper. While 'nature' is something that has clearly run through the whole history of art – if only as a debased acanthus leaf on a Roman temple – with Wordsworth's pantheism and Turner's landscapes it became part of that supreme elevation of the Imagination of which Coleridge had written. It became in fact, very nearly, God. As such it revolutionized the English mind, leaving us with a good deal of artistic rubbish in our art galleries and streets, but also with a sensitivity and awareness which would have been impossible in the Georgian era. In the nineteenth century something happened to the human mind – a change of an almost biological order, a change in Man's attitude to the whole world outside himself. One has only to imagine, say, Christopher Wren trying to read Proust, to get the point.

Now although this sensitivity and awareness is first found in the Lakeland poets and in the landscape painters, in a Romantic attitude to Nature, by mid-century that attitude was transformed by John Ruskin, and linked by him, curiously enough, to Architecture.

Ruskin will be examined more fully in his place. In 1843 he gave the world the first of his five volumes of *Modern Painters*. Begun as a defence of Turner and of 'truth to Nature' in painting, it ended as a marvellous and bewitching dissertation upon clouds, skies, seas, alpine peaks, twigs and dewdrops. *The Stones of Venice* followed ten years later.

The impact of Ruskin upon Victorian England was shattering. If Regency England had succumbed to the idyllic charms of the Picturesque, this in fact had meant little more than the informal glade, a richer foliage and serpentine lakes. Now, with Ruskin, it was realized that Wordsworth had meant something more than lyrical sweetness, Turner something more than a Royal Academy sensation. A Victorian God rode upon the storm. He was to be sought in the depths of the seas or upon the mountains, also in the life and art of those men who had lived closest to Him and to Nature, who had built grey Gothic towers in northern forests, or the golden caverns of St Mark's upon the salt tides of Venetian lagoons.

It was an amazing discovery. If, in real life, it seemed to lead only to amateur watercolours, to touring the Trossachs, Killarney, the Swiss Alps or Florentine churches ... it nevertheless revealed new worlds, worlds within which the Cotswold village or the French cathedral both had their place.

The issue had become a moral one. Architecture, whether Classic or Gothic, could never again be merely a polite stylistic essay. Gothic Architecture, God, Man, Nature, Imagination and Art were now all to be inextricably intertwined in a complete Ruskinian world.

The distant, the strange, the curious and the evocative ... the characters Dickens found in cockney lanes, or Thackeray below-stairs in Belgravia; the whorl of a shell picked up on the shore, or the mystery of a fossil; Rochester's mad wife raving through the night; young Thomas Hardy sketching Gothic details, or Newman's bewitching sermons in the crowded, gas-lit aisles of St Mary's; Rossetti's odd and phthisic Pre-Raphaelite women ... all things that are strange, curious and evocative.

The nature of a Romantic Movement can be seen in many ways: Romanticism and Liberty, Romanticism and Low Life, Romanticism and Nature, Romanticism and the Macabre, Romanticism and

Science, and so on. Strangest, most evocative of all – and indeed embracing all the others – was Romanticism and the Middle Ages. It was Froude who said that the eighteenth century had a sense of history so inadequate that it saw the Middle Ages only as a great uncharted ocean, with the single great rock of the Norman Conquest, the cathedrals drifting around like hulks. A century later almost every medieval church and castle had been labelled, visited, restored ... the Middle Ages, with industrial capitalism, was the twin obsession of the age. One may ask, Why? And the answer, in effect, is an exploration of the Gothic Revival.

3

The Gothic Revival: Phase One

For the last four hundred years most of the architecture of Europe has been a series of stylistic revivals. Neither the Classic architecture of Greece and Rome, nor the Gothic architecture of the Middle Ages were always slavishly copied – freely treated, they were even, now and again, the inspiration for works of genius – but the architectural vocabulary of the Renaissance and the Baroque was at least as Roman as the architectural vocabulary of Victorian England was Medieval.

Once the Renaissance – under the hands of Brunelleschi and Alberti – had flowered in the fertile soil of Medicean Florence, then the great natural architectures were doomed to pass out of this world forever. These were the architectures, the last total works of Man within which function, structure and beauty were inextricably combined into a kind of architectural trinity. These golden ages – Periclean Athens, Angevin France, Tudor England – could never happen again.

The Renaissance, as it spread from Florence to Rome, and then over the Alps in the next century to France, and so to England, had been so much more than a 'revival of learning', so much more architecturally than a change of style. It had been a tremendous revolution, taking in its giant stride both the Reformation and the Age of Discovery. Feudalism and Ecclesiasticism had died together. Patronage had shifted from Church to Crown. Out of a dying feudalism there were gradually born, through three centuries, a secular world of sovereign states. Feudal lords, after all, cannot build empires, and so as an Atlantic world replaced a Mediterranean one, it was the seaboard states with their fleets and armies – Spain, Holland, England – who took over the torch. A sovereign, secular, mercantile and aristocratic art means, in effect, snob culture and a courtier or merchant class. When opera, painting and furniture replaced the Gregorian chant, the ballad and the coloured roofs and screens of village churches, then the professional architect, with his array of antique scholarship, the Grand Tour and the drawing-board replaced the masons, carvers and limners of the cathedrals. The Renaissance had been hailed as a great dawn; it was Victor Hugo who called it a great sunset.

If the reasons for the artificial revival of a classical architecture in Renaissance Italy are explicable and justifiable, then the reasons for a revival of a medieval architecture in Victorian England are equally explicable, equally justifiable. Perhaps both, viewed on the high plane of history, are regrettable. It is, however, a mere fiction of modern scholars to assume that the real and true architecture of Europe is only that which runs through the Renaissance, Mannerism and Baroque – from, say, Brunelleschi to Soane – while all medieval architecture is no more than an embarrassing prelude, nineteenth-century architecture no more than a lapse from grace.

Stylistic revivals – whether in Italy or England – can never again give us Parthenons, Torcellos or Lavenhams. There can be no more miracles. Stylistic revivals are, in themselves, regrettable. That a revival in Italy should be classic, that a revival in England should be Gothic were, however, facts of life – as natural as they were inevitable.

Medieval or Gothic architecture had not been just a style of pointed arches, pinnacles and filigree. With its high vaults and systems of abutment it had been the world's greatest engineering. This engineering had had its seat and origin in the Île-de-France, in the great cathedrals around Paris. It had had its branches in Spain, in Flanders and England. It had crossed the Alps, but south of the Alps it had never sent down any tap root. While the Gothic arch, the pinnacle and all the filigree are there, at least after a fashion, in Milan, that is the farthest point south. The engineering and the whole intangible mystique of Medievalism are missing, while Rome itself is a wholly Pagan or Baroque city without a single Gothic church. Through all those medieval centuries Rome had slept. 'The Gothic North' is not an empty phrase.

Through the Middle Ages Rome had slept – the cattle had been stabled in the palace courts, the sheep had grazed in the Forum, the temples had crumbled. But it had been a sleep, not a death – a hiatus.

In the fifteenth century, when the Renaissance set alight the cultural fires of Florence, Italian eyes had opened upon the scene of an Imperial heritage. The ruins, the roads, the institutions of the Empire were all around. If the Medicis, Sforzas, Borgias had to build themselves churches and palaces – with Alberti, Michelangelo, Borromini and the rest to do it for them – then the manner in which they built could, quite clearly, be only Roman. In the England of Queen Victoria that situation was reversed.

The seed of Renaissance architecture germinated easily in the soil of Italy, the seed of Gothic germinated as easily in the soil of England. Both the continuity and importance of Renaissance and Classical architecture in England is now exaggerated. Admittedly, the two centuries of Anglo-Palladian and Anglo-Baroque – from Inigo Jones to Soane – are not an unimportant chapter in the history of architecture, but they do after all represent only an imported art. They are part only of an aristocratic culture, not part of the long vernacular, universal, native or national art of the English people – the grey tower of the village church or minster, the high roof of the manor or the farm. If one must study the Palladian, then better Palladio than Jones; if one must study the Baroque, then better Michelangelo than Wren. In England there are other things ... and in a fumbling way the Victorians knew this quite well.

The fine gold thread of romanticism and medievalism had never quite vanished from the rich tapestry of English history. The first fine flush of the Renaissance in England had shown itself quite palpably as an exotic and imported style. All those Elizabethan 'prodigy houses', Longleat, Wollaton and the rest, are after all medieval castles – all turrets, mullions and leaded lights – with a few fashionable Italianate flourishes only in the fireplaces and doorways.

But that was not all. A culture is a unity of all the arts. The English Renaissance, having secularized culture and thus liberated the mind, had thereby promoted literature and drama to replace architecture as the 'dominant' of the Elizabethan Age. Almost within a generation of the building of the Gothic Chapels Royal – those last works of 'total' architecture – Shakespeare was conforming to an Italianate fashion by giving nearly half his plays Italian settings. Far more significantly, almost all the other half were a celebration of medieval kingship.

For the golden thread ran on. Through the seventeenth and eighteenth centuries, when St Paul's Baroque dome was rising among the even more Baroque City steeples, when Vanbrugh's Roman arches were already dominating the Cotswold slopes at Blenheim, when a hundred Palladian houses were being set in English parks, when the Establishment had given to the cathedrals the sobriquet 'Gothic' to mark their crudity ... even then the golden thread gleams.

Vanbrugh's most Baroque, most Roman buildings, are essentially as Romantic as they are Baroque, as medieval as they are Roman ... Seaton Delaval, for all its rusticated Doric, is like some rugged fragment from the Wars of the Roses; Blenheim, with its four corner towers, is a veritable castle. This, however, would seem to have been a matter of temperament, not style. For it was not Vanbrugh but Wren himself who could, however unwillingly, actually build Gothic pinnacles and even fan-vaulting of a kind. He did so at St Mary, Aldermary, in 1702–4 [16].

16 Christopher Wren: St Mary, Aldermary

The lovely Gothic tower at St Mary's, Warwick, was designed and built in 1698 – when Wren was already old – by a Baptist master mason. The great vaulted stair at Christ Church, Oxford, was built in 1640, the year Inigo Jones began his Palladian front at Wilton. St John's College, built about 1630, was used two centuries later by the Tractarians to prove, absurdly enough, that Archbishop Laud's Anglo-Catholicism had also made of him the first Gothic Revivalist. In fact there are other seventeenth-century buildings in Oxford more Gothic by far.

Were all these curious things just oddly belated 'hang-overs' from the Middle Ages, were they the first swallows of the Gothic Revival summer, or were they just a native romanticism overriding a current fashion? Perhaps a little of all three ... but mainly the last, since that sort of romantic view of Gothic, a partiality for the vernacular, runs through our whole culture.

If Shakespeare could never, perhaps, have quite touched upon 'Gothic', he came very near it. Over and above that procession of heraldic kings, and far nearer his heart than Italy, had been certain aspects of romanticism. There had been yellow sands and caverns deep, fairy woods and blasted heaths, the moonlit battlements of Elsinore. And Milton, civil servant in a Puritan administration within a Baroque epoch, wrote no lines so familiar as those where, so clearly, he feels the spirit of Gothic:

> But let my due feet never fail,
>   To walk the studious Cloisters pale,
> And love the high-embowed Roof,
>   With antick Pillars massy proof,
> And storied Windows richly dight,
>   Casting a dimm religious light.

But then there never was a time when English literature was not saturated with the Gothic spirit and the ghosts of its long past. Malory and Froissart had, after all, cast a romantic gleam upon chivalry and knights in armour – both Gothic things – while chivalry and knights were still part of the real world. The Gothic Revival was born not in early Victorian churches – that was its consummation – but in the flame of the English spirit.

Back in the sixteenth century, a generation before the architectural word 'Gothic' had been coined, Francis Bacon could say that it was 'a reverend thing to see an ancient castle or building not in decay'. The love of delicious decay came a little later, but no Italian could have written that ... only Bacon, supreme intellect of the High Renaissance, but child also of the grey Gothic North.

When the crescents and terraces of Georgian Bath were fresh from the builders' hands, and when the Baroque of Rome had run its course, Thomas Gray, in England, could invoke not only the whole spirit of bucolic romanticism, but also 'the long-drawn aisle and fretted vault', while disdaining the 'storied urn and animated bust' of the Palladian tombs.

To the long tale of mutilation by both reformers and puritans, the Restoration added the dismantling of the castles. Love of decay – with its whole apparatus of ruins, owls, ivy and moonlight – became yet another factor in the Gothic complex. At about the time when Gray was composing his Elegy, William Mickle, in the woods of Roslin Castle, could write:

> August and hoary, o'er the sloping dale,
>   The gothic abbey rears its sculptur'd towers.
> Dull through the roof resounds the whistling gale;
>   Dark solitude among the pillars low'rs.

Well before the close of the eighteenth century, in a book much read by Shelley, *Les Ruines, ou Méditation sur les Révolutions des Empires*, Chasseboeuf de Volney wrote of 'Solitary ruins, sacred Tombs'. He wrote: 'All hail ye mouldering and silent walls. To you I address my Invocation!'

For two hundred years – at least until the 'Gothic style' was accepted for the Houses of Parliament in 1836 – the word 'Gothic' was ambivalent. For the eccentric or for the poet it was always a suggestive word – redolent with all manner of dreams and passions. Officially, so to speak, it remained a term of contempt, a synonym for the barbaric as opposed to the 'polite'. 'O! more than Gothic Ignorance,' wrote Fielding.

All the same, if rain poured through the thatch of village churches, it was in those churches that nobility and peasants worshipped together, that their ancestors rested. If the cathedrals crumbled, their mutilated loveliness unregarded, those sculptur'd towers rose undeniably – almost a challenge – above the roofs of little county towns. If it was the fashion to live in a Palladian mansion, the ancient castle was the insignia of lineage. If medieval history was a wilderness, since the days of Leland and Camden local antiquities had been part of a gentleman's equipment.

Deep in English soil, all the time, the sap of Gothic was being nourished. A Gothic Revival, sooner or later, was quite inevitable. It came at first tentatively and oddly; then, in the early years of the Queen's reign, like an avalanche.

Tentatively and oddly ... the golden thread in the tapestry, or what Sir Kenneth Clark has called 'the brackish stream', had been preserved until the middle of the eighteenth century: partly by this spirit of the vernacular; partly by sheer *Survival* – surviving pockets here and there of old-style masons – partly by a confused respect for Norman blood and genealogy; partly by a love of antiquity and archaeology; partly by a wallowing in Gothic 'horror' and decay.

17 Robert Adam *et al.*: Strawberry Hill, exterior

These things prepared the ground. The real *Revival*, when it came, was a matter of taste and conviction. It cannot be said to have truly existed until Horace Walpole (1717–97) began in 1750 to 'gothicize' Strawberry Hill, his villa at Twickenham [17, 18]. He had already endeared himself to romantic circles with *The Castle of Otranto: a Gothic Story*. (This was the first of the 'Gothic novels'.) Walpole claimed that it was written almost subconsciously from a dream, a dream of a gigantic hand in armour seen on the uppermost banister of a great staircase. It was a nonsensical romance of horror, exaggerated sensibility and the paraphernalia of ruin. It was a great success. It is not, however, Walpole's story that matters; it is his house.

Those other aspects of the Gothic spirit – conservatism, snobbery, antiquity – had each had its own manifestations. These were either those curious instances of Survival – that tower at Warwick or the stair at Christ Church – or foolish trifles such as sham ruins, grottoes, follies, gazebos and the like. Sanderson Miller had done very well out of designing sham ruins such as the one in the park at Hagley [19] –

18 Robert Adam *et al.*: Strawberry Hill, the library

nicely balanced by a Doric temple on the opposite hill. It was an authentic-looking fragment, described by Walpole as bearing 'the true rust of the Barons' wars'. Yet another architect, Batty Langley – with a severe classical background – believed that Gothic, like classic, must be amenable to some sort of Vitruvian rule. In his *Gothic Architecture Improved* (1742) he put forward a whole series of designs for small Gothic buildings – Umbrellos, Temples, Pavilions and the like – suitable for the adornment of gentlemen's parks.

These things were trifles. Strawberry Hill is the real forerunner of Victorian Gothic. It is a real attempt to revive a medieval style for a major building. As such it could never have been wholly successful. It fails most where it tries hardest.

Strawberry Hill was a four-square Georgian house. Neither in plan nor in structure was it suitable for 'gothicizing'. That was not important for at that date neither plan nor structure were considered to be part of a style. Externally Strawberry Hill has some twisted brick chimneys – the influence of near-by Hampton Court? – some wooden Gothic window frames and a battlemented parapet. That is all. It was internally that Walpole ran riot.

Strawberry Hill inspired Walpole with romantic excitement. It was his brain-child with which he tinkered year after year. In its own day it became the first 'stately home' to which the public were admitted

19 Sanderson Miller: Sham ruin, Hagley

20 Frontispiece: Bentley's 'Gray'. *By the middle of the eighteenth century the romanticism that was eventually to produce the full flood of the Gothic Revival was evident in décor, in the novel and in verse. Here in architectural embellishment, in the ancient lineage of armorial bearings and in the simple tools of the peasant, are some of the ingredients of 'Gothick'.*

for a fee. The monastic hall and great stair were a most suitable setting for the author of a Gothic 'best-seller'. Walpole employed more than one designer. He first engaged Richard Bentley. Bentley, significantly, had already illustrated an edition of Gray's poems [20]. He impressed upon Strawberry Hill its main character. The lanthorn, the stair and the great chimney-piece all bear the mark of a fanciful, graceful and, indeed, Rococo interpretation of Gothic. It has nothing whatever to do with the Middle Ages – its charm is the elegant charm of the eighteenth century.

Then Bentley dropped out – he was lazy – to be replaced by Chute. There now began, under Walpole's supervision, a process of cribbing from ancient folios. The archaeological replaced the graceful. Chute and Walpole worked very hard. Specific medieval tombs, altars and screens can still be recognized in the doorways, bookcases and ceilings of Strawberry Hill ... even though often to the wrong scale, and only in plaster. This was a most ominous process. It was also a most Victorian process. With so little real Gothic actually surveyed it was not possible in Walpole's day to copy very much very accurately. The attempt was made. For nearly a century the ideal of archaeological accuracy was to haunt the Gothic Revival ... and to do it no good.

After Strawberry Hill the Gothic mansions came thick and fast. There is a kind of architect who can today, without a blush, offer the local authority or the Royal Fine Art Commission, a neo-Georgian or modern façade ... as required. Nothing could so emphasize the 'professional' or commercial status of the eighteenth-century architect as the cynicism with which, while preaching classical elegance and correctness, he could – as required – turn his hand to Gothic. The immaculate Soane was not guiltless; Chambers gave us a sham castle; Robert Adam several; James Wyatt actually preferred Gothic, while Nash may be said to have run his office with Classic and Gothic departments. The complete eclecticism, with which the Victorians have been so firmly labelled, was founded in the Augustan Age.

The numerous Gothic mansions fall roughly into two classes. The first is the restored or sham Norman keep, such as Arundel, Belvoir [21], Eastnor or Windsor, which demonstrated the lineage rather than the taste of the owner. About the time of the Napoleonic Wars – with the influence of Waverley at its height – the country was littered with

21 James Wyatt: Belvoir Castle. *By the turn of the century romantic Gothic had spread. It was no longer just for churches, let alone for the 'follies' of eccentric patrons; it was fashionable. The great aristocratic families were busy gothicizing their houses or even building new castles. Macaulay could refer to ' Belvoir's lordly terraces'.*

22 James Wyatt: Fonthill Abbey, central octagon

**23 James Wyatt: Fonthill Abbey,
view from the park**

such castles. Only the large sash-windows in the turrets let the cat out of the bag.

The second class of mansion was more truly Gothic, more poetic, more uncomfortable, and far more amusing. It is the loosely planned, highly romantic monastic pile. It was James Wyatt who left us two such monuments – Fonthill, 1796–1807 and Ashridge, 1808–13. Of Fonthill only a fragment remains. From engravings, and by comparison with Ashridge, we may deduce how exciting it was.

The rich, egregious, egotistical and perverted William Beckford, having duly forestalled Byron in launching the myth of 'the wicked lord', instructed Wyatt to build him a ruined convent, later to evolve into a mansion in the likeness of an abbey. On the far slopes of Salisbury Plain lies the lovely site to which Beckford added the eight miles of encircling wall, the woods and the lakes. Here, gimcrack, rambling, vast and impossible, Wyatt raised the house with its great staircase entrance, its vaulted octagonal hall [22], its galleries and its fragile tower more than 276 feet high [23].

Fonthill, for all its Arabian Nights quality, was the first building of the Gothic Revival to show some realization that Gothic is *not* a mere stylistic essay, *not* just an alternative style, *not* a mere matter of pointing the arches and cusping the plaster ceilings. Fonthill was a real, if crazy, attempt to recapture that romantic grouping of towers, turrets, stairs and cloisters that had been the essence of the old abbeys. Forty years later Pugin could dismiss the symmetry of the Palace at Westminster as 'Greek bones in Gothic clothing', Pugin disliked Wyatt but he could never have said that of Fonthill.

Fonthill was the house of a madman – footmen in monks' habits, perfumed coal in the grates, orchestras in the moonlit woods, black magic in the chapel – but it was, like the whole of the Gothic Revival, an attempt to realize a dream. It overrode the archaeology of Walpole in order to set an enchanted convent in Wiltshire woods. That it should fail was inevitable. It failed because it was built too quickly and too flimsily, and showed it. Its detail, like all Gothic detail of that date, was thin and uncraftsmanlike. Walpole understood Gothic as a series of forms; Wyatt as a system of planning and massing. No one yet understood it either as a structure or as an expression of a way of life that had for ever passed from the world ... Ruskin and Morris were still half a century over the horizon. Fonthill was a form of Gothic that the Victorians could have enjoyed – even while criticizing it – but it was one which neither Chambers nor Adam nor Nash could even begin to understand. It reveals James Wyatt as a bridge between the age of the eccentrics and their 'follies' and the true Revival of the nineteenth century.

In our own time, in spite of the victory of modern architecture, it is still inevitable that in most people's minds Gothic should be associated with churches. Real Gothic, after all, had been the style of the cathedrals. That attitude had not been the attitude of the eighteenth century. The Tractarian Movement, however, was to be a watershed after which nothing was ever the same again. We live in a secular age but we live this side, as it were, of the Victorian era with all its religious revivals, its fervent piety and its great wave of church-building. Walpole, Beckford and the rest did not see Gothic like that. To them it was a mere item in the history of Taste. Very few Georgian churches had been built in Gothic – slim, elegant, fragile, even charming – but they were wholly un-medieval, and they were very few.

Until about 1820 the Gothic Revival was almost wholly a matter of private houses – an upper-class whim. In any case, between, say, 1760 and 1820, very few churches, were built in any style. Vast populated areas – the industrial towns and the sprawling London suburbs – were without churches. This was most disturbing. It was bad in itself; it was also an invitation to dissenters to build chapels. The nineteenth-century gentry might let the poor starve and rot, but were always prepared to do something for their salvation. It was under pressure from the Church Building Society, as well as from fear lest a godless people might also be a revolutionary people, that Parliament in 1818 passed the Church Building Act. One hundred and seventy-four churches were built. The style, if it could be called such, was an economical Gothic ... at least the arches were pointed! Nash, Smirke, Soane, all did designs of a sort for the Commissioners.

A young, unknown classicist, Charles Barry, also turned his hand to Gothic – at Stand in Lancashire (All Saints, 1822) and at Brighton (St Peter's, 1824). The only real monument to the Church Building Act, however, is St Luke's, Chelsea (1820) by James Savage [24] ... an

24 James Savage: St Luke's, Chelsea. *One of the churches built by the Parliamentary Commissioners from 'the million pound fund'. This was subsidized Gothic, and although one of the more lavish examples it clearly shows economy in the detail.*

indubitable piece of Perpendicular Gothic, with real stone vaults and flying buttresses. It is almost Victorian.

However shoddy these Parliamentary churches might be, they were a portent. Until after the Napoleonic Wars the Gothic style had been officially regarded as a harmless toy for the romantic or the rich. Churches were quite a different matter. With the Church Building Act of 1818 – for better or worse – Gothic was placed upon the statute book as a recognized style.

That was something. At least it showed a serious state of mind about architecture. Between cheap churches for the slums and important public buildings, however, a great gulf was still fixed. The British Museum which was begun in 1823, the Bank of England which was being built from 1788 to 1833, the National Gallery from 1834 to 1838 and the Royal Exchange which was begun in 1842 were all, as a matter of course, buildings of the Classic Revival. Gothic, as a historical and a national style, was nevertheless to receive its accolade just two years before the Queen's accession.

*

Standing amid the rich foliage patterns of St James's Park, one can behold the most enchanting urban scene in the world; also one of the oddest. As one faces that famous skyline of towers and minarets – the Foreign Office, the Life Guards and Whitehall Court – one can glimpse, away to the left, the long, classical horizontality of Nash's Carlton House Terrace. Away to the right, above the roofs of Storey's Gate, is the most extraordinary group of towers in the world ... the eighteenth-century Gothic of the Abbey and the nineteenth-century Gothic of the Palace of Westminster. Between the completion of Nash's Terrace and the beginning of Barry's Palace there lie little more than ten years. In the history of taste alone, it is an incredible *volte-face*. Actually, in the history of a people it symbolizes far more than that – it symbolizes the change from an aristocratic to a democratic art.

On the night of 16 October 1834, Charles Barry was returning from Brighton. As the coach crossed the Downs a glow was seen in the sky over London. Later they met the post-boys with the news that the Palace of Westminster was on fire. They reached London to find Westminster Hall standing unharmed in the smoking ruins. The old

Parliament House of St Stephen and the old ramshackle law courts were all destroyed. It is said that as Barry looked upon the scene he was already thinking of the opportunity it might offer to a young architect.

Out of those ashes, in due course, arose two phoenixes – the new Houses of Parliament and, thirty years later in the Strand, the new Courts of Justice – two major monuments of the Gothic Revival and of the Victorian Age.

After the destruction of the Palace a Parliamentary Commission was set up. It was decided, in 1835, to hold a competition. It was also decided that the design must be in the Gothic or Elizabethan style.

On the face of it this was an astonishing decision. The lords and gentlemen of the Commission, many of them, must have owned Palladian mansions or Georgian town houses. They must, all of them, have had a classical education. They must, some of them, have been upon the Grand Tour. On the other hand they must, almost all of them, have prayed in village churches and spent their impressionable years in Gothic quadrangles. They had, unwillingly, studied Virgil and

25 Charles Barry and A.W.N.Pugin: Houses of Parliament

Horace; they had, willingly, soaked themselves in the long romantic tradition of English literature.

Another thing: after Waterloo England had begun to emerge into greatness and prosperity. The Reform Bill, passed three years earlier, showed the growth of the industrial towns – with their peculiar mixture of philistinism, liberalism and romanticism. The Nation, controlled for generations by a few great Whig families, now became aware of itself; it basked in the glow of patriotism. Searching, inevitably, for the myth of its own golden age, it found it in Gothic architecture – the 'English style'. That Westminster Abbey, with the tombs of medieval kings, was just across the road, also weighed with the Commission. That both the kings and the Abbey were mainly French could, in the exalted mood of 1835, be easily forgotten. Medievalism as a facet of patriotism was as much in the air as was Gothic as a facet of culture. The decision of the Commission was not, after all, so very astonishing. Indeed, it was inevitable. Gothic, in 1835, became the official style of England [25].

4

The Gothic Revival: Phase Two

Augustus Welby Pugin (1812–52) was far more important than his buildings. If Barry's Houses of Parliament stand for the official recognition of the Gothic Revival as 'the English Style' – a manifestation of patriotism – then **Pugin** brought about its more serious recognition as 'the Christian Style' – a manifestation of piety [26].

26 A.W.N.Pugin: *Apology for the Revival of Christian Architecture in England.* Frontispiece

Born of a French father – one of Nash's best draftsmen – and of a strictly evangelical mother, Pugin's home was cruel and narrow. When he duly revolted he took with him his dual inheritance of an artistic temperament and a religious passion, and in both he remained a fanatic to the end of his short life. By the time he was twenty-five he had designed scenery for Drury Lane – altering the history of English stagecraft – had married and tragically buried his first wife; built his own 'grange'; bought a boat – 'the only things worth living for are a boat and Christian architecture' – sketched the churches of France and Flanders, entered the Roman Catholic Church, and published at his own expense his first book, *Contrasts, or a Parallel between the Noble Edifices of the Fourteenth and Fifteenth Centuries and similar buildings of the present day* (1836).

Contrasts was an explosive work. Side by side, page after page, in fine pen drawings, the thirteenth century and the nineteenth century were compared ... reservoir with well-head, the minster with the bethel, the almshouse with the workhouse, the hostelry with the gin palace, the manor with the suburban villa, and so on. It was called unfair; in fact it was devastating.

This book brought Pugin his first commissions. In 1837 an English Catholic architect was in a peculiar position. The Roman Catholics were an obscure sect, half-persecuted, half-tolerated, generally feared. Newman's conversion was still ten years off, but the trickle of converts had begun – Pugin was one of them. These converts – the 'New Catholics' – in so far as they cared about architecture at all were more Roman than Rome. They were the core of the Catholic Revival, but that neo-baroque dome of the Brompton Oratory in the Brompton Road was their sign-manual.

The 'Old Catholics' – Wardours, Vavasours, Throckmortons – were those old families who, having survived the centuries since the Reformation, still worshipped privately in private chapels. The Church of Christ would triumph in the end; they could bide their time. They resented the upheaval of the Catholic Revival; they resented the converts; they resented Pugin.

It was to the 'English Catholics', to a small clique of eccentric millionaires that Pugin had to turn – Charles Scarisbrick, March Phillipps de Lisle, the Earl of Shrewsbury. These men, like Pugin, evoked the dream of an old Gothic England with all its Gothic glories. It was not just the altar, the chalice and the patten that were to be the tabernacle for the sacrament; it was, as of old, to be the whole church. Gothic Revival architecture was moving into another phase. In the eighteenth century it had been a dilettante's folly; with the Commissioners' churches and the Palace at Westminster it became a serious style – a valid alternative to classicism. Now, with Pugin, it became a means of grace, a way to salvation. As Kenneth Clark has written: 'The stream in which Walpole dabbled and Beckford splashed so exuberantly was to wash away the sins of the English Church.'

For Charles Scarisbrick – as much a part of the Rochester myth of the 'rich recluse' as Beckford had been of the 'wicked lord' – Pugin built in Lancashire a Gothic mansion [27, 28]. In the wild marshes, backed by woodlands, Scarisbrick still stands with its single tall spire. It is rich with oak carving, coloured vaulting and wallpapers that forestall William Morris ... there is much that is reminiscent of the best that was yet to come at Westminster. In the mansion where Charles Scarisbrick lived in gloom and isolation, Pugin gave his client as fair a house as any Catholic squire had lived in since the Reformation.

27 A.W.N.Pugin: Scarisbrick Hall, exterior

Scarisbrick did not revive the tradition of the English vernacular, as we see it in manors or farms – that had to await the generation of Shaw and Lutyens. Pugin here applied to domestic architecture all the ornament and carving that had once belonged to the architecture of the church. The house is as replete with pinnacles, finials and tracery as any fourteenth-century lady-chapel. It is all wildly wrong – as were Strawberry Hill and Fonthill – but unlike them it is well done on its own terms. Pugin himself would have called it simply 'the real thing' ... it was a step forward; the Gothic Revival was moving from childhood to adolescence.

In the last brief years of Pugin's life, John Talbot, Earl of Shrewsbury, spent about three hundred thousand – say, two million in modern money – on Pugin churches. There were many of them – most of them in 'the Pugin country' north of Stafford – and the money was spread more thinly than Pugin liked. Lord Shrewsbury's munificence, moreover, included St Chad's Cathedral in Birmingham [29], and his own seat, Alton Towers [30].

Alton – those 'gorgeous halls' wherein Lord Shrewsbury occupied a whitewashed cell – is one of the most curious, most fantastic houses in England. Pugin's work included the apartments of the earl's daughter, the Princess Pamphilia-Doria, the great stair, the dining-hall, the armoury and the chapel. The chapel was virtually a church. It was there that Pugin's second wife was received into the One Fold with ceremonies which, it was said, might have caused comment in the Middle Ages. Alton could have been just one more Beckfordian folly; in fact, for all its fantasy, the Gothic style is here so established, so rich, so solid and self-assured, that Alton bears unmistakably the Victorian stamp.

Pugin's churches also bear that stamp, as well as the stamp of Pugin. Catholic theology, ecclesiology and lack of funds combined to create the typical Pugin church. The rood-screen – symbolic division betwen laity and priesthood – was never neglected. On the screen, the chancel and the altar Pugin lavished his rich fourteenth-century carving, his colour and his Minton tiles ... the nave, as a consequence, had to be thin and austere. 'Pugin,' it was said, 'starved his roof to gild his altar.' It was true. It was done for reasons of the deepest piety, but it may explain why his churches are, for us, less interesting than the man.

In thirty years Pugin did the work of ten men. At the time when he was pouring out designs and drawings for Alton, for Scarisbrick, for a dozen churches, and for March Phillipps de Lisle's Trappist monastery in Charnwood Forest, he was producing as many drawings again for the Palace at Westminster.

Charles Barry had won that competition, and won it fairly with a brilliant plan. With the Lord Chamberlain's House and the Peers at one end of the building, the Speaker and the Commons at the other end, the great Octagonal Lobby common to both, and the libraries and committee rooms on the quiet of the river front, it was both a classical and an efficient plan. It is like a diagram of the British Constitution.

But at heart Barry was no gothicist. His real monument will always be that lovely Italian palazzo in Pall Mall, the Reform Club, and the Travellers' Club next door. Barry could plan, he could organize, he could deal with committees. The high romantic dream that embraced the fretted richness of the late Middle Ages was beyond him. He

31 Charles Barry and A.W.N. Pugin:
Houses of Parliament, St Stephen's Chapel

needed Pugin. Today he would have made him a partner. In fact he picked his brains and treated him as an assistant. The old and bitter Victorian controversy – 'Who was the real architect of the Houses of Parliament?' – need not concern us. The architect was Barry, but almost all that is best and most enchanting was Pugin's.

Had Pugin actually planned the Houses of Parliament we should doubtless have been landed with some lovely but incompetent sequence of conventual cloisters. As it is, the vaulted lobbies, the former Commons Chamber, the thrones and the canopies, and what is perhaps the loveliest room of the nineteenth century, the Peers' Library, are all Pugin's [33]. So also was much of the external detail – all that fine Perpendicular panelling, together with the silhouette of the great towers [34]. Of course it was all 'sham Gothic', but those towers, more than anything else, are still symbols of Victorian London. They are also, in certain moods and lights, of quite breathtaking beauty.

If Pugin's patrons, 'the English Catholics' with their Gothic dream,

32 Charles Barry and A.W.N. Pugin:
Houses of Parliament, Royal Gallery

were few; if 'the New Catholics' – the converts – were Italianate in their tastes – those converts had left behind them in the English Church a great wave of Gothicism. Gothic was, from now on, the Anglican style, above all the style of the Tractarians, of the High Church party.

Before Keble had preached his famous Oxford Assize sermon – on the apostasy of an Erastian Church – the word 'ecclesiology' was hardly known. Then, suddenly, it is everywhere. Gothic was entering another phase. Having already become the style of the pious, it was now found to be the style of the sacerdotal – the only possible style for the correct and functional setting of the full rubric and ritual of Anglo-Catholicism.

With intense undergraduate enthusiasm the Cambridge Camden Society was founded in 1839 for the furtherance of a strict ecclesiology. The design of chancel, side-chapel and aisles – both as symbols and as spaces for certain rituals – became an aspect of Gothic not less important than its history or its ornament.

The plain Protestant preaching house which had been the basis of

33 Charles Barry and A.W.N. Pugin: Houses of Parliament, main staircase

34 Charles Barry and A.W.N. Pugin: Houses of Parliament, view from Henry VII's Chapel

35 William Butterfield: All Saint's, Margaret Street. *The polychromatic interior – marble, Minton tiles and glazed brick – is typically Butterfield; typical of his determination to turn Gothic into 'a modern style' using modern material.*

the English church ever since Wren had designed the churches of the City, was suddenly transmuted, not only into the Gothic style, but into a Gothic plan for – very nearly – a Gothic service. The doctrine of the Camden Society was a revival of the full Catholic ritual. Amenable architects sought the Society's advice. Other architects were anathema; they were placed upon a black list. The Society's favourite architect – to use their own phrase – was Butterfield, one of the few to survive the Society's inquisitorial interference.

William Butterfield (1814–1900), although the darling of the Camden Society, was in some ways hardly a medievalist at all. An essay (1945) on Butterfield, by Sir John Summerson, bears the significant sub-title, 'The Glory of Ugliness'. While accepting Gothic as the only conceivable style, Butterfield was concerned with it mainly as a vehicle for honest building. He was a Gothic functionalist. He delighted in that kind of ugliness – the ugliness of ruthless realism and of the rejection of sentiment – that one finds in the earlier Pre-Raphaelite paintings such as Millais's *Christ in the house of his Parents* or, fifty years later, in early functional architecture. Butterfield's Gothic detail was often ugly. It was ugly because it was coarse, uncompromising, useful rather than pretty. He designed foliated capitals with vigour; he designed chimney flues with meticulous care, and with equal pleasure.

When Butterfield built All Saints, Margaret Street (1849–59) [35] or Keble College Chapel (1873) [36] it would never have occurred to him not to build in the Gothic style. Both buildings were, indeed, excessively stylistic, to the point of being bizarre in their rich detail. But to Butterfield's mind it was not the style that mattered; that was taken for granted.

William Butterfield, in appearance and in fact, was a stern, tight-lipped, narrow and puritanical Anglican. His whole being was concentrated upon his celibate rule of life and upon the integrity of his work. To the whole of his design, to the hidden and mundane construction, as well as to the ornament, he applied those high standards that Ruskin was already demanding of the craftsman. Butterfield's building operations were as highly disciplined as had been those of the Middle Ages – prayer and the rule of silence were the accompaniment of manual labour.

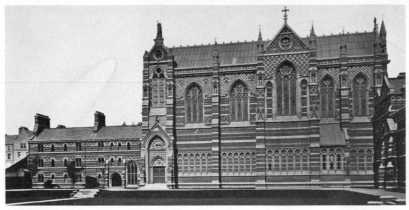

36 William Butterfield: Keble College Chapel

It was all this that led Butterfield on to a further idea, a most pregnant one. He believed that he was living in a new and a very revolutionary age. At the peak of Victorian industrialism it would have been difficult not to have believed that, but Butterfield went further. He believed that Gothic, also, must be made part of that age, that it must be made into a modern style, fit for its own time. The grey dream of a poetic Age of Chivalry must be abandoned for the sake of hardness and reality. The highest tribute, after all, that one could pay to the Age of Faith was to build Gothic well. The quality of the mortar or of the lead gutters was as much a part of the piety of church building as the carving on the reredos. Moreover, all that was good and new in a new age must be made use of. The frescoes of the medieval churches had long since faded from the walls. Paint was ephemeral, but it was no longer necessary to use it. Marble, coloured and glazed brick, Minton tiles and terra-cotta could all be pressed into God's service. They could be made to form a bold scheme of decoration, iconography and symbolism. They would last forever. Thus, paradoxically, in the rich, gaudy Gothic of Keble or All Saints, did Butterfield create what he felt to be a 'modern style' – and thus was born a most curious kind of functionalism.

Butterfield, therefore, although he comes rather early in the story

37 William Butterfield: St Saviour's Vicarage, Coalpit Heath. *This shows Butterfield's restraint when he was not building to the glory of God. It also shows him as a 'craftsman' architect – a worthy forerunner of men like Philip Webb and Lethaby.*

of the Gothic Revival, and is outwardly almost violently Gothic, is in fact a strangely unexpected bridge between the Age of Wyatt and ourselves. In time he is almost half-way between the two.

If, under the influence of Morris and the Arts and Crafts Movement, the later Gothic Revivalists were to repudiate both a strictly archaeological approach, as well as Butterfield's crude colouring and coarse detail ... Butterfield's influence was nevertheless profound. It was profound in secular as well as ecclesiastical architecture. If Butterfield had been the darling of the Camden Society, then Gilbert Scott was the darling of the Establishment.

Sir Gilbert Scott, R.A. (1810–77) – is remembered as Lord Palmerston's antagonist in the 'Battle of the Styles'. Sooner or later that clash between a classically educated patron and a Gothic Revivalist was bound to happen. Barry, in spite of the acceptance of the style at Westminster, had been shabbily treated and badly paid. Faces had been barely saved. Between Scott and Palmerston there could be no face-saving. Each stood for a different culture, almost for a different century. Scott had designed the Foreign Office in an odd amalgam of French and Venetian Gothic. Palmerston would tolerate no such 'monastery'. Scott, 'for the sake of his wife and little ones', thereupon produced a classically adorned façade.

To that comedy we owe something – William Morris's realization that the stylistic battle had become worse than ludicrous, a symbol of a fragmented culture. But it was not that fiasco that raised Scott to such official eminence.

The Prince Consort had died in 1861. Early Victorianism died with him ... to be replaced by something more confident, more absolute. Before Albert's death it had been decided that the profits from 'his' Exhibition – the Great Exhibition of 1851 – should initiate through land purchase and grants, that huge complex of museums, colleges and institutes that lies between Cromwell Road and Kensington Gore. A century later, that complex is still being added to ... the most astonishing collection of bizarre Victoriana that we possess. That any memorial to Albert should be an addition to that collection was only fit. That his widow should have ideas more grandiose than the nation would pay for, was only likely. As those ideas came to be diluted, so also did the contribution of Sir Gilbert Scott dwindle. His 'Gothic'

Albert Hall, intended to be part of the Memorial, was abandoned for lack of funds; a speculative scheme was substituted, acoustically bad but designed by two Sappers.

Scott's Albert Memorial, apart from its history as a wildly fluctuating thermometer of taste, is as good an insignia of High Victorianism as one could have [38]. Its site is splendid and symbolic. Looking down, as it does, upon the Albert Hall, it carries the colour and the texture of Kensington architecture across the road into the Gardens. Eastwards it closes the axis of the long, broad avenue that was once the site of the Crystal Palace.

Scott was the secular and worldly obverse of the Butterfield medal. The same determination to make Gothic a 'modern style', to use colourful, new and permanent materials, is evident. Mosaic, marble, pink granite, gilded bronze, glazed tiles and a hidden iron skeleton – as well as a vast basement – are the 'modern' aspects of the Albert Memorial. The iconography, the literal representation of sentiment, the excess and the pathos are the Victorian aspects. Only the cusps and the pointed arches remain to uphold the Gothic aspects. Scott's idea – to reproduce a small altar tabernacle on a large scale – has long since been forgotten. It may have been an absurd idea in itself; that it could be done worse is forever demonstrated in the Waverley monument in Edinburgh.

The Albert Memorial sculpture belongs to the High Victorian epoch – not the Early Victorian. It is utterly uninhibited. It has forgotten all elegance. It veers from the realistic – almost Pre-Raphaelite – portraits of abstract Virtues, to equally literal, equally realistic symbols of the Four Continents – all camels, elephants and bison. The whole thing is set upon a high plinth. The principles of *The Seven Lamps* should have kept this 'structural' element plain and strong; in fact it is deeply carved with a portrait gallery of the Great – from Moses to Millais.

Scott's technique is superb, his self-assurance complete. His art – granted certain premises that are no longer granted – is also superb. It is certainly consistent. The violent polychromy and the vigorous shapes are consistent with each other. They are consistent with the equally rich and vigorous pattern of the foliage and the shrubbery that is their setting. The Albert Memorial is not small. It holds its own above the tall, mature trees of Hyde Park and Kensington Gardens. The only inscription was the single word 'Albert'. As Lytton Strachey remarked: 'as a means of identification this has proved sufficient'.

Gilbert Scott was the supreme model of a Samuel Smiles self-made man ... with all the vigour and all the lack of subtlety that one would expect. It was by the Albert Memorial that he wished to be remembered. That egregious masterpiece is unlikely to be forgotten; as architecture, however, it is the St Pancras Hotel that is most likely to be regarded as a symbol, not only of Scott himself, but of that whole mid-Victorian epoch [39]. It combines in one building the romantic aspirations, the stylistic display and the solid philistinism of the sixties. With its variegated and strident materials, its tremendously Gothic skyline and its ramped and terraced base, it is a most positive piece of design not a mere essay in the Gothic style.

It was in some ways the greatest achievement of High Gothic. Its appeal was terrific. It became a tourist attraction. It was fashionable to spend a night there amid the whistling of the locomotives and the rattle of the cabs and carts on granite sets. It was painted against the sunset. In spite of the piety of the age it was also appropriate that the major monument of those boom years should have been a railway hotel rather than a church. It was, perhaps, an even more suitable gateway to the Midland Railway than Hardwick's Doric Propylaea at Euston had been to the London and Birmingham.

In one other way also – although this was not realized at the time – St Pancras was symbolic. The station itself, designed by W. H. Barlow (1812–1902) is the finest of the great iron train sheds. Scott's hotel is the most extreme epitome of the Gothic Revival. The two together are the perfect expression of that tragic schizophrenia that is Victorianism. The northern railway stations were built on the northern rim of the town, all strung out along the Marylebone and Euston Roads. To the south of St Pancras are the well-ordered eighteenth-century Bloomsbury squares, to the north a disordered wilderness of sidings and squalid streets. The hotel and the Station sum up that disorder. Each may be superb, but the curve of the iron roof sweeps ruthlessly across the fretted arches of the Gothic windows in the Hotel. That was accepted at the time without comment. The station was 'Useful' and the hotel was 'Art'. That points clearly to the

divorce between Engineering – an obsession with large-scale structure – and Architecture – an obsession with style and ornament.

Counting alterations and restorations, over a thousand buildings passed through Scott's office in about forty years. He must have employed an army of assistants, but the Victorian apprentices, the Martin Chuzzlewits, were given small chance to strike out on their own. Only one of any account emerged from the Scott office – George Edmund Street.

The largest of all neo-Gothic buildings, Giles Scott's cathedral at Liverpool, nearly a hundred years after the building of his grandfather's hotel, is still unfinished; yet seventy years ago Heathcote Statham could describe Street's Royal Courts of Justice in the Strand, as 'the grave of Modern Gothic'. They were nothing of the kind – the Gothic Revival died hard – but the Law Courts do demonstrate the defects as well as the merits of Victorian architecture – the obstinate refusal to subordinate in any way the style of the building to practical needs.

The English Catholics and the High Church Party could live very well in a world of their own. Deliberately spurning the roaring booming Victorian Age, they could dream dreams of a Gothic world that never was on land or sea. Abasing themselves before the mystery of the Sacrament, as men had not done since the Reformation, the whole panoply of Medieval architecture was their natural home. An artificially revived architecture was the corollary of an artificially revived religion. It was the far harder task of Barry, Scott, Waterhouse or Street to apply the principles of the Gothic style to large public buildings – buildings that were necessarily complex in plan, structure and equipment. Barry, with Pugin's help, had pulled it off at Westminster ... even so, and significantly, he had grave trouble with the heating. Scott, in his vulgar way, pulled it off at St Pancras ... even so, and significantly, he had to ignore that lovely iron roof. Street pulled it off in the Law Courts ... even so, and significantly, he had grave trouble with the acoustics. With Waterhouse all practical problems were overcome. There were now no inhibitions over either style or decoration. The professional expertise of the whole thing was such that one forgets completely that this is a 'revived' style. It has forgotten all about its medieval ancestry and belongs as completely to the nineteenth century as did, say, Wren to the seventeenth or Le Corbusier to the twentieth. If any one Victorian architect may be said to have 'dug the grave of the Gothic Revival', it was Waterhouse, not Street.

The fire which in 1834 had destroyed the old Houses of Parliament had also destroyed the conglomeration of law courts which had, through the centuries, gathered themselves around Westminster Hall. An entirely new 'Royal Courts of Justice' had become necessary, to be built at Temple Bar, nearer to the Inns of Court. Street, against eleven competitors, and in a competition (1866) which, although not actually corrupt, was extraordinary, was awarded first place. Barry, whose elevations were superior to Street's, was fobbed off with a promise that he should build the National Gallery – a promise fortunately broken. Street had to design his Law Courts for more than one site, but on the site in the Strand, at Temple Bar, they are still a conspicuous monument.

Pugin might have given us something more poetic, but he was dead. Butterfield might have given us something more bizarre, but he never went in for competitions. Waterhouse would have been more efficient, Scott more popular. In the event Street gave us a building which is typically Victorian in that it is compounded of great qualities and great defects. Among judges and barristers it has always been a bad joke. Baron Huddleston, advising upon the design of a provincial Assize Court said, that 'everything that Street did should be avoided'. The acoustics – the almost complete inaudibility of witnesses – must have caused many miscarriages of justice. The courts, corridors and stairs are dark.

On the other hand, Street's building has magnificent features. It carried the Gothic Revival a stage further ... it took it from the drawing-board into the street, acknowledging the relationship of architecture to what we would now call 'town-planning'. Long symmetrical façades cannot be seen in narrow streets – an elementary fact still ignored. The lovely scenery of the medieval towns – gables and towers on to alleys and narrow ways – cannot have been accidental. The Law Courts were large, but Street considered each façade, not as a single academic study, but as a series of groups – towers, turrets, judges' portal, arcade and so on – each forming, as it were, a little

41 G. E. Street: Royal Courts of Justice, the Carey Street front
42 G. E. Street: Royal Courts of Justice, the Great Hall

architectural scene, each separately valid in the sharp perspective of the street – whether Bell Yard, Carey Street or the Strand [40, 41].

George Edmund Street also succeeded where his competitors had failed. In the heart of his plan he embedded the big Central Hall of the Courts, the *salle des pas perdus* [42]. Superficially this Hall is a thirteenth-century vaulted nave; it is also impressive in its own right. The late H. S. Goodhart-Rendel called it 'the noblest room of the century, perhaps the noblest room in England'. This is an exaggeration; it is not a gross exaggeration.

One other architect had offered the judges a far more poetic, far less practical design than Street's. This was William Burges (1827–81).

Burges never emulated the commercial success of a Scott or a Waterhouse, but he was not the least of the real artists of High Victorian Gothic. He was as self-consciously medieval in his own life as Pugin had been in all his fanaticism, or Butterfield in his pietistic celibacy. Burges's sketch-books, like those of Villard de Honnecourt in the thirteenth century, were of vellum. His inkstand was in the likeness of an elephant and his own portcullis actually worked. He wrote essays on the Retabulum in Westminster Abbey, on the Confessor's Chair and on Henry vii's Tomb. A figure in medieval costume always had to be worked into his design somewhere or other – as over the lavatory basins in his Melbury Road house.

Burges's imaginative and eccentric disposition could, however, erupt into commonsense and into an athletic vigour of design. Those contradictory characteristics of the Victorian Age, the aggressive and the charming, he combined in his person and in his buildings. Both qualities are necessary to an effective skyline, and this Burges achieved again and again.

His largest composition was at Trinity College, Hartford, Connecticut (1873) where the long lines of Brown Stone 'medieval' quadrangles are punctuated by a whole series of towers, turrets, flèches and pavilions. This could have been an apt description of the Law Courts had they been designed by Burges and not by Street.

Burges's array of romantic castellated towers belonged to the medieval missal – such as that of Paul de Limbourg – rather than to the real medieval world. In their fullest complement – redolent of arches and dungeons – they are to be found at Cardiff Castle – the mansion that Burges restored for the Marquis of Bute. 'Restored' is an understatement; by the time Burges had finished with it, the Castle, with its fantastically rich interiors, had become one of the most gorgeous houses of its time [43, 44].

The Cathedral at Cork – designed in a very muscular sort of twelfth-century French Gothic – demonstrates the riches which the Protestant Ascendancy of Ireland were prepared to lavish upon a religious building in the seventies. This Cathedral, like all Burges's work, shows his love of the dramatic skyline and of the view from afar. The three big spires – with detail obviously coarsened to 'read' from a distance – dominate the town of Cork as one sails in from the sea. Within is a

43 William Burges: Cardiff Castle, the hall. *Burges is, for some reason, better known for his own house in Melbury Road, Kensington – perhaps because of the often illustrated Gothic lavatory basins. Actually that house was full of richness. Here, at Cardiff, its promise is fulfilled. For the Marquis of Bute, Burges here created some of the most colourful interiors of the whole Gothic Revival.*

great wealth of craftsmanship and colour – roof, pulpit, screen and so on – nearly all traceable to Burges's own hand. His work shows his skill; it also shows signs of his close friendship with Morris, Burne-Jones and the Pre-Raphaelites. In some ways, therefore, the work of Burges is ahead of its time. In his personal care for craftsmanship, his personal execution of detail, he belongs to the neo-Gothics of the next generation, to the generation of, say, Philip Webb, Bodley, Temple Moore or Comper, to the Arts and Crafts Movement which was born under the star of William Morris.

45 G. M. Kemp: Scott Memorial. *Although built about a quarter of a century before the Albert Memorial, the canopy or* baldacchino, *over the statue, makes a comparison inevitable. The Albert Memorial is by far the more competent and self-assured. This Memorial stands well in the Prince's Street Gardens, and is a foil to its classical neighbours, but the scale is appalling ... the pinnacles are as high as the double-decker buses, and Walter Scott is quite crushed by the architecture above him.*

46 Deane and Woodward: University Museum, Oxford. *Externally this is pure Venetian Gothic and is directly inspired by Ruskin's* Stones of Venice. *Internally the iron and glass roof was anathema to Ruskin and caused his resignation as consultant.*

47 J.L. Pearson: St Augustine's, Kilburn. *Pearson's work is all scholarly, showing a real archaeological knowledge of the phases of Gothic development. This is no exception. It is also an example of the 'symbolic' Gothic of the seventies, when a spire was a finger pointing to heaven.*

48 T.G. Jackson: Brasenose College. *This kind of secular Gothic, or domestic Tudor, was the forerunner of innumerable collegiate efforts of the same kind, right into our own day. It was also one of the first of innumerable Cotswold pastiches.*

49 G.F.Bodley: Church at Hoar Cross. *This remarkable and very beautiful little church – privately built by the Meynell family – may be considered the first example of 'neo-Gothic' as opposed to Gothic Revival building. It is a completely free use of the style, the emphasis being upon design rather than upon historical accuracy. It had a great influence upon Liverpool Cathedral.*

50 J.L.Pearson: The Cathedral, Truro. *In spite of a fine skyline, the emphasis is upon historical accuracy rather than beauty. Correctitude is taken to the point where the Gothic style is made to change as the building rises – as if, medieval-fashion, it had taken generations, not a few years, to build. Once accept the premise and it is well done.*

 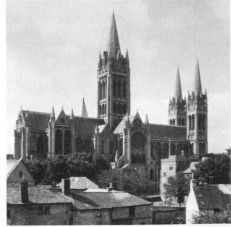

5

The Crystal Palace and the Engineers

We have traced the romantic theory of English architecture from the age of 'follies' in the eighteenth century to the High Gothic of the mid-Victorian era. So far as the professional architect was concerned that romanticism was the main stream of thought. Architecture, however, is not merely what the architects choose to call 'architecture'. It is all building, it is the creation of almost any kind of shelter for man's activities, and it is the making of cities.

In that hundred years of industrial capitalism the professional architect played, relatively, a very small part. It was an age of unprecedented growth, an age of rapacious landlordism and speculative building, of large industrial structures. That, not 'architecture', was the building programme of the age. It was a programme unprecedented in history, and upon that programme the architect, with all his stylistic and High Art obsessions, his academic inhibitions and his professional snobbery, turned his back.

The era of Nash's Regent Street had all ended in a cloud of dubious scandal, suspicions of professional corruption and the involvement of the architect in the finance of his own projects. The Institute of British Architects had been founded to rescue the architect from this state of affairs, to give him what we would now call 'status'. It succeeded, and in succeeding did irreparable harm to architecture. It emphasized the elevation on the drawing-board and upon the wall of the Royal Academy; it divorced the architect from the facts of life.

The romantics – not only the architects but the philosophers and poets – were important only in the long run. Seen in the perspective of the great world – the world of statesmen, industrialists and landlords – they were, the whole lot of them, very small beer indeed. They were little more than a rebel and Bohemian clique – the Victorian beatniks. What, after all, was the real Bible of the nineteenth century if not Bagehot's *English Constitution* (1867) – the text-book that was on the desk of every prince and every minister?

I maintain [wrote Bagehot], that Parliament ought to embody the public opinion of the English; and certainly that opinion is much more fixed by its property than its mind. The 'too clever by half' people who live in 'Bohemia' ought to have no more influence in Parliament than they have in England, and they can scarcely have less.

Who were these 'too clever by half' people – so despised by the Establishment? They were the Puseyites, they were the agnostics, they were the romantic poets, they were the Pre-Raphaelites, they were perhaps even the philanthropists; certainly they were the Gothic Revival architects ... these were the unacceptable elements of Society. The Court, the nobility and squirearchy, the new urban landlords, the manufacturers, the railway tycoons and the engineers ... these were the acceptable elements. Drawing-room society might strike a different pose ... toying with culture as a series of fashions, as 'taste', but in the last and the real analysis, railway shares would always matter more than pointed arches. That iron roof at St Pancras destroying so ruthlessly the Gothic detail which was as elaborate on the back of the hotel as on the front, was a wonderful symbol. There lay the great dichotomy of the Victorian Age. It was a dichotomy that had to be resolved before, once again in history, a rational and an imaginative architecture could emerge. The iron roof and the Gothic dream had each their contribution to make. The conflict between them had, sooner or later, to be resolved. There had, somehow, to be an architecture that would take account of both.

*

All London is astir, and some part of all the world. I am sitting in my quiet room, hearing the birds sing, and about to enter on the true beginning of the second part of my Venetian work. May God help me to finish it to His Glory and Man's good.

That was the entry in John Ruskin's diary for 1 May 1851. That was the morning when Queen Victoria opened the Great International Exhibition in the Crystal Palace, in Hyde Park. So far as *Stones of Venice* went, Ruskin's was an exalted mood; so far as the Crystal

52 Ford Madox Brown: *Work*

Palace went it was one of priggish contempt. Carlyle, too, was writing from Dumfries to Jane Welsh, about 'this Kensington Bazaar'. On the other hand, Thackeray, novelist of the philistines, had written an ode. It was all about the bright arcades of this palace for a fairy prince. It was also about England's bloodless conquests – toiling engines, tunnels and whirring looms.

1851 was not an age of transition; it was the celebration of the triumph of the English ironmaster. The landed Regency bucks, the stiff unbending lords, were being replaced by railway kings and cotton merchants. There was a 'Manchester philosophy'. The gay stucco spas were giving way to the warehouses, to the square miles of marshalling yard, to the Rhonda Valley, to county gaols and to the Black Country. On the northern rim of London, in 1810, they had made the Regent's Park, with its elegant terraces; less than a generation later they were making the great stations to link the capital with the industrial North. Toiling engines, whirring looms, *and* the elegant and magical glass palace for the fairy prince, utility and romance, cash and sentiment, cruelty and piety ... that was the quintessence of the age. That was the perverse and contradictory Victorian Age from which modern architecture, and indeed our whole visual world, has somehow had to emerge.

When once the island's coal measures had been linked by water or by iron to the deep estuaries, the stage was set for rebuilding London and ruling the world. The international character of the 1851 Exhibition was not due to a cosmopolitan or enlightened interest in foreigners; it was a patronizing gesture from a *Herrenvolk*, fearless of competition. The technical and industrial revolution of the nineteenth century – with all its consequences for society and for history and for art – can be studied only in England. There it can be pinned down, like some biological specimen, and dissected.

As that industrial Empire, with its slave economy, took shape, there emerged Disraeli's 'two nations' – one rebuilding London for the other. It can all be seen in Ford Madox Brown's *Work* (1863) [52] – the elegant and idle rich set against the fine strong navvies ... the first generation of agricultural workers, the John Bulls, to drift into the towns. Without bloodshed, but with an infinity of suffering, infant mortality and child labour, there was shattered the older rural and

53 Workers' cottages, Newcastle on Tyne

113

aristocratic society – the society that had had only two kinds of architectures, that of the landlord and that of the tenant. Now the looms in the cottage parlours – of which George Eliot had written in the Coventry of her childhood – vanished; the assembly line came into being.

True, there was another side to the picture – the Victorian Age of our own nostalgia. We can recall wistfully quiet scenes: country rectories on autumn afternoons, the 'sprigged muslin in Kensington Gardens', or the dreaming, empty spaces of the High at Oxford, with the shopkeepers putting up the shutters for the long vacation. But much more was it an age of brilliant lights, deep darks, tremendous energy and flashing melodrama. The black smoke above the new cities was drama enough, but symbolically we must see it also drifting across the farmlands of George III, and across the parks of the England of the Regent. The Satanic Mills lay very close under the moors of Wuthering Heights [53]. Only in Victoria's England could Renishaw and the Derbyshire coal-fields share the same landscape; only in Victoria's England could Nasmyth's steam-hammer be enshrined in a fairy palace in Hyde Park.

The great industrial and technical revolution was not a torrent; it was a Niagara. For the new philistine it meant hard cash. He might soothe his conscience with Sabbatarianism or philanthropy, or even by building churches, but by and large he was punch drunk with cash. To offset his materialism – often indeed his gluttony – he might pretend to, or even feel, a hunger for Romance. He might devour the novels of Walter Scott or even join the High Church. But for all that he could never begin to understand that lost tradition of taste and style that had, for the eighteenth century, mattered so much. Those few, aristocrats and antiquarians, last relics of the days of the Grand Tour, to whom that classical tradition still mattered, were swamped. The scholarly architect – at least as the world had known him since the first dawn of the Renaissance – was at last in eclipse. He had gone out, not with a bang but with a whimper, with Nash and Soane. In this new virile landscape of viaducts and raw embankments, lying beneath smoky skies, the broad highway lay open to the engineers … and they took it.

It was not just that Telford designed some good bridges; he built

54 W.Cubitt: Mimram Viaduct, Welwyn. *The Cubitts were a versatile family. Thomas designed upper-class houses in Belgravia; Lewis designed a remarkable terminus to the Northern Line at King's Cross; William designed this splendid viaduct on the same line – an example of good architecture achieved through pure functionalism.*

55 Robert Stephenson: Britannia Bridge

the Holyhead Road – the first by-pass – in an effort to revolutionize Anglo-Irish communications. It was not just that Brunel built Paddington [56] and Temple Meads; he built the whole Great Western and thus made possible mining in South Wales and seaside holidays in Devonshire. The railways, like the motor-car, were both hated and used. They were a technical change and a social revolution [57, 58].

And the railways were not all. We have only to look at the black nineteenth-century chunks on the grey mosaic of the London Ordnance Survey – stations, sidings, gasworks, docks, warehouses, workhouses, prisons and hospitals – to see that it was a world whose structural achievements, as it liked to boast, really did outweigh those of the Pharaohs or Caesars. Yet, somehow, it is the architect who suddenly becomes a dim figure ... retreating into his ivory tower and his irrelevant Gothic dreams.

The tragedy of that divided Victorian society was twofold. First, its dual nature kept it forever from the highest peaks of achievement. The golden ages of Parthenons or Ravennas had not only long since passed from the world; they were also inconsistent with this

56 W.P.Frith: *The Railway Station. This painting – like Turner's* Rain, Steam and Speed *– is one of the few instances where the world of art and the world of industry and utility, came to terms with each other. The station is recognizably Paddington. With the baggage on top of the carriages and the bustle, how near is this early railway scene to the yard of the posting inn?*

combination of railway booms and earnest romanticism. Second, it was tragic because, with the best intentions, it could never itself quite make out what had gone wrong. The age was fascinated by its own mines, pumps, bridges and tunnels. It had no doubts about either their magic or their novelty, but it also felt some curious moral duty to regard them only as a source of useful wealth whereby something quite different could be encouraged – the 'Fine Arts', meaning sometimes the worst sculpture, painting and architecture ever known.

What the Age could not see – it was too near to itself – was that the destruction of an aristocracy, a priesthood and a peasantry – patronage, inspiration, craftsmanship – that had begun four hundred years before, was now completing itself and that the vacuum must be filled. It must be filled, not by incidental fashions in style, still less by the 'Fine Arts', but as always by the age's own essence. That essence was *structure*, engineering ... and upon structure and engineering the architects had turned their backs.

Of course when either half of the age was being true to itself, when railway kings were swinging brick viaducts over the Dee Valley, or

57 J. Hawkshaw: Cannon Street Station

58 Queen Victoria's Saloon on the Royal Train. *A collaboration between engineers and upholsterers. In spite of the lush design there were no conveniences; small lavatories had to be built at the side of the track for the long journey to Balmoral. Somewhere in the upholstery a handle was concealed whereby the Queen could modify the speed of the train.*

59 Bazalgette: Victoria Embankment, London

building four-level fly-overs at Stockport, or when, on the other hand, Turner was painting, say, the *Sun of Venice Going to Sea*, or Pugin was devising the scarlet and gold of the House of Lords – then, as an age, it *almost* takes its place in the great succession of world cultures.

The artist, finding his inspiration in Nature, in his dreams and the passion of his social protest; *or* the conformist engineer jumping on the band-wagon of his time, had each their great moments. The painters, poets and architects could still matter a little as an official opposition, but mainly because they were an underground force reshaping their world for the distant future and for us. In the great roaring fifties, however, they must have seemed in their ivory towers to have mattered only a very little. Wordsworth's *Excursion*, Carlyle's *Past and Present*, Ruskin's *Seven Lamps*, Dickens's *Dombey and Son* – with its Camden Town railway scenes – Pugin's *Contrasts*, the Tractarian Movement, the Pre-Raphaelite Brotherhood or Morris's *News from Nowhere*, were all arrows let fly from the ivory tower against grime and cash. But for the real architect there could never be that ivory tower; and out in the cold hard world, under the smoky skies and with a slave economy to hand, the Brunels and the Telfords were too busy and too prosperous to bother with him ... much.

Just now and again the two worlds met. The poet might glimpse romance in 'the ringing grooves of change' and Martin might paint his fantasies of Chaos and Old Night, from sketches made in the Black Country at dusk. Bell Scott painted the industrial scene – *Iron and Coal* – as part of a historical series at Wallington Hall in Northumberland; while Turner saw a vision from the train at Maidenhead and called it *Rain, Steam and Speed.* Then, too, now and again, as on the Conway Bridge, the engineers might condescend to battlements or machicolations. But on the whole any appeasement in that cold war was rare. It can never have seemed very likely that those turbulent years of poverty and wealth, squalor and elegance, would leave behind them any symbol of their monstrous two-headed nature. In the event they did; that symbol was the Great Exhibition of 1851, and the Crystal Palace in which it was housed [60].

Whether we see the Crystal Palace as an elegant shelter for the display of engines, or as a utilitarian iron structure for housing bad sculpture, it was a miracle. As, indeed, was the Great Exhibition itself. On the face of it, it ought never to have happened. The industrialists were too busy and too prosperous to need an exhibition; the aristocracy were too comfortable, too remote, to bother with it; while the intellectuals can have seen no reason at all for celebrating the triumph of filth and cruelty. It is, indeed, difficult to conceive of any neutral guiding force which could bring together those warring elements officially described as 'Machinery, Science and Taste'. This force must be patriotic but not insular; it must be hard-working; it had to be earnest about economics, romantic about science and

60 J. Paxton: Crystal Palace

61 J. Paxton: Crystal Palace, general view of interior
62 J. Paxton: Crystal Palace, west nave and transept

scientific about art. Clearly, therefore, it had to be German. Prince Albert, since his marriage, had been popular neither with the aristocracy nor the mob. He was solemn and he didn't hunt; but every dog has his day, and 1 May 1851 was most emphatically Albert's.

The Exhibition was his conception, the Crystal Palace his child. Without Albert's support against the entrenched professionalism of the engineers, as well as against popular suspicion, Joseph Paxton – then known only as a designer of fountains and greenhouses – would by now have been forgotten.

The whole form and structure of the Crystal Palace was dictated by expediency. It is an illustration, if ever there was one, of the thesis that only through inspired obedience to all the circumstances of a moment does an artist succeed. The Crystal Palace was poised magnificently and accurately in mid-century. In its transparent Regency elegance – the first realization that metal and glass could have positive aesthetic qualities of their own [61, 62] – there lay the perfect setting for the rather Winterhalter scene of 1 May 1851, when the Queen opened the Exhibition. That scene, with its high-stepping, curved-necked guardsmen's horses, was all a flurry of red velvet, ostrich plumes and little girls in pantalettes ... yet it was the model of the new Liverpool docks that the royal party first inspected. For all its attenuated elegance, the Crystal Palace could never really have belonged to the age of Nash or Soane. Its elegance was somehow begotten by Paxton out of the Palm House at Kew [63] and the Chatsworth conservatory which he had already designed for his ducal master. Essentially, however, the Crystal Palace belonged to the new age; it was a triumph for big Midland contractors. The conservatories were only collateral; the real ancestors were the iron train halls – Euston, St Pancras [64] or Newcastle Central – and the big Paris markets.

A building reveals its designer as mercilessly as it does its era. The more one studies the Crystal Palace the more plain does it become that Joseph Paxton was a man of taste but not education. His opinions upon everything were orthodox; his genius lay in an infinite capacity for taking pains. He was not, perhaps, the most eminent of Victorians; he was certainly the most typical. He was self-made – or, as the Queen called him, 'a common gardener's boy'. He was a model of the domestic virtues, but moved easily among the aristocracy. He

63 Decimus Burton and Richard Turner: Palm House at Kew. *In realizing the architectural possibilities of the big conservatory, priority must be given to Paxton with the 'Great Stove' at Chatsworth – a few years earlier than Kew. But that Decimus Burton, a classical architect, should collaborate on this building shows that, already, the glass house was not beneath the notice of the distinguished professional.*

64 W. H. Barlow and R. M. Ordish: St Pancras Station

was romantic about the exotic plants he grew; he was practical about girders and money. He dabbled confidently in both railway shares *and* the cultivation of giant water-lilies. The Crystal Palace was by Euston Station out of *Lilia Victoria Regia*.

By the middle of 1850 Albert and his Commissioners who had been labouring for months to realize their great conception for a great exhibition were now in despair. Brunel had designed them an Exhibition building of brick, with an iron dome. It could not be properly lit. It was ugly – a pure chunk of the industrial North. It would cost more to pull down than it had cost to put up. It was fuel for the fire of those who, from the start, had violently opposed Albert's whole scheme as a desecration of the Park.

It was on 7 June 1850, during a board meeting of the Midland Railway, that Joseph Paxton (1801–65) – now a director – made his famous blotting-paper doodle [65]. Nine days later the Chatsworth Estate Office had turned that doodle into a vast set of plans and calculations. A problem had been solved. It is not always realized how essential it was that the Crystal Palace should be 'crystal' – that its walls and roof really should be ninety-five per cent glass. In 1851, with

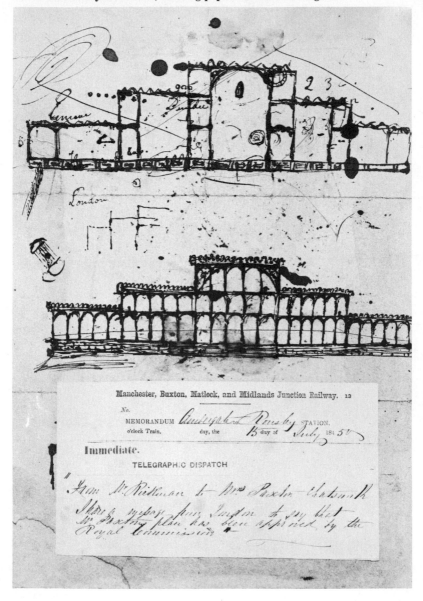

the incandescent mantle still forty years over the horizon, the artificial lighting of a building one-third of a mile long – as long as Portland Place and twice as wide – could not be attempted. The Crystal Palace always closed at dusk. Another essential was lightness in weight – the thin iron frames filled with glass, unlike brick walls, required no massive foundations. A third essential was speed. An agreement between the Commissioners, the engineers and the glass manufacturers, was signed on 16 July 1850. On 31 January 1851 the building was handed over, ready for the reception of exhibits. Between those two dates lies the first miracle of prefabrication. It was one which, for nearly a hundred years, was without a sequel.

A miracle ... because the essence of prefabrication is full preparation. The work is on the drawing-board and in the factory rather than on the site. Paxton's draftsmen turned out, in those nine days, hundreds of sheets of exquisite and entirely original details. Even the beautifully designed columns and joints which Brunel had used on the big stations, were no sort of precedent for this building. There were also the details for the many ingenious devices – the famous little trucks which ran on the gutter rails of the roof, sitting in which the glaziers and painters could do their work. There were the mechanically controlled louvres for ventilation – the opposition had prophesied that everyone would be roasted alive in this giant greenhouse. There were the very graceful iron stairs to the galleries. All these things, like the iron frames of the main structure, were on a strict module, so that even the fence round the site could ultimately go down as floorboards. Paxton prepared everything and thought of everything.

It was a building without a sequel, but only in the sense that full prefabrication – the making of a building in a factory rather than on the site – had to await our own day. The Crystal Palace, if we forget its curved roofs, does, after all, remind us of some modern schools or of factories for the new light industries. It is not surprising: one of its functions – to let in light – and its technology – metal and glass panels bolted together – were both modern. The economy, the lightness and the elegance thus achieved were an architectural revolution. For centuries, stone by stone, buildings had been laboriously piled up from the ground, even the stones themselves being shaped on the site. Today it is a commonplace to assemble the component parts of a building; Paxton was the inventor of this far-reaching revolution in architecture. In history there have been only two such revolutions. All architecture belongs to one or other of only three main structural families. One, *trabeated*, where the beam or slab rests directly, with dead load, upon the column or wall. Stonehenge and the Parthenon and most suburban houses belong to this family. Two, *arcuated*, where the space is spanned by a number of wedge-shaped stones, or voussoirs, holding each other in position whether as arch, vault or dome, and exerting outward thrust against the wall or against the buttress. All the Roman and post-Roman styles (Romanesque, Gothic, Baroque, etc.) belong to this family. Three, *metallic* – the architecture of iron, steel or reinforced concrete which has its own structural laws.

The Crystal Palace was not of course the first building of iron. On the contrary it crowned a wonderful series, including the great stations such as Euston (1836), King's Cross (1850) [66] and also the great bridges from Coalbrookdale (1777) on, including the Clifton Suspension Bridge (1836) and buildings such as Bunning's London Coal Exchange (1847) where the iron was much enriched with ornament [67]. The Crystal Palace, however, was the first structure to attempt seriously the transference of metallic building from the purely 'utilitarian' field to that of 'architecture' – where the whole building was not just ornamented but was an aesthetic concept. As such it had to be taken seriously. It may not have been the sort of architecture which either the 'Classic' or the 'Gothic' professionals could be expected to take seriously, but at least it may be said that it broke entirely new ground.

A few years later, in 1855, in the Oxford Museum, Deane and Woodward were using an ornate Gothic cast-iron roof inside an otherwise Venetian Gothic stone building [68]. Then came a whole series of such buildings – some frankly functional, others re-interpreting the historical styles in iron. Brunel's iron roof at Paddington (1852) had been merely embellished by Digby Wyatt with a little Moorish decoration; Boileau's St Eugène in Paris (1854), however, although wholly of iron, was also wholly Gothic. Far more significant was the *Halle des Machines*, built for the Paris Exhibition of 1889. This building had a span of three hundred and eighty-five feet. It owed nothing whatever to historical styles and was highly architectural. It showed a

66 Lewis Cubitt: King's Cross Station. *Most of the big stations – Euston, St Pancras, Newcastle and many others – were sooner or later disguised by hotels or other 'architectural' frontispieces, as if their functional magnificence was something to be ashamed of. Here, in the two big arches, 'arrival' and 'departure' is frank recognition of function, and something of the big scale of viaducts and bridges is brought through on to the street.*

67 J.B.Bunning: The Coal Exchange. *This was another way of looking at that contro-versial new material – iron. If indeed architecture was 'ornamented building' then iron, too, like stone, must have ornament. A dubious theory, but superbly done. (Now demolished.)*

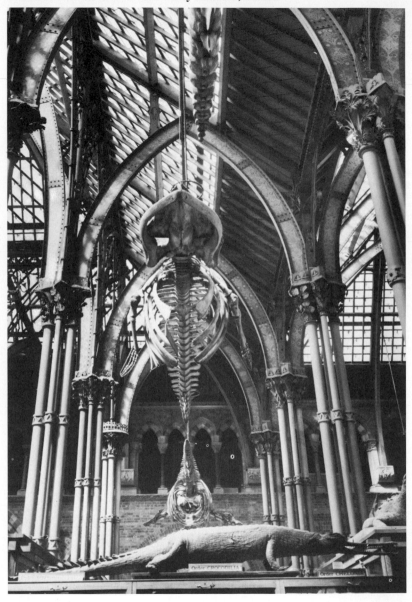

superb sense of its material and was modern in the full meaning of that word.

In some quarters – in spite of the example of the Crystal Palace – all this building in iron was inevitably very disturbing. It seemed to make nonsense of any principles that had been laid down upon the basis of history. Ruskin had, for instance, acted as adviser to Deane and Woodward in the building of the Oxford Museum. The employment of a genuine Irish peasant craftsman to carve the stone ornament, did nothing to mitigate his disgust, or to deter his resignation, in the matter of the iron roof. *The Stones of Venice* (1851–3) had, after all, opened with a definition of what 'separates architecture from a wasp's nest, a rat hole or a railway station'. Viollet-le-Duc had referred to market halls and railway stations as being, after all, 'only sheds'. After the success of the Crystal Palace they all had to think again, so that Viollet-le-Duc, in his *Entretiens* of 1863 now conceived the idea of a complete iron-framed building, while even Ruskin could write of a time when new architectural laws must emerge 'adapted to metallic construction'. Gilbert Scott had said, as early as 1858, that 'this triumph ... opens out a perfectly new field for architectural development'.

That 'development', however, was left severely to others. Some sort of modern architecture might, by mid-century, have become undeniable ... but how they all hated it! It had to be left, indeed, to another generation, almost to another century, actually to welcome it, to understand it and to transmute it, if they could, into something which men would have to admit was a real architecture – as real in its own way as any in history. But it was to be over forty years before, in the roaring Chicago of the nineties, Sullivan and the young Lloyd Wright would break through to 'something new under the sun' – to the first of the steel-framed skyscrapers of urban America.

6

High Victorianism

The phrase 'High Victorianism' has never been defined. Like the words 'romantic' or 'classic' it is better undefined. We can sense some more subtle meaning if we leave it without a narrow definition.

We have seen how the Gothic Revival ran through a number of phases. First – far back in the eighteenth century – there had been the 'follies', sham castles and other appendages of the Picturesque. Second there had been the use of Gothic – a mean and thin Gothic – for those economically built 'Commissioners' Churches'. Thirdly, and almost at the same time, there was the use of the style to express ancient lineage and Norman blood – 'castles' such as Eastnor, Belvoir or Eaton Hall, and those that stand decaying in the great demesnes of Ireland. Fourthly, Thomas Rickman, in his *Attempt to Discriminate the Styles of English Architecture* (1817), saw Gothic as a study for the archaeologist, giving it those absurd but useful divisions, Early English, Decorated or Perpendicular; while the Camden Society at Cambridge studied the style, also archaeologically but mainly as a vehicle for ecclesiology or ritual – the Society's favourite architects being Butterfield and Street. Pugin, meanwhile, riding high on the Catholic Emancipation Act and the Catholic Revival, saw Gothic as a 'Christian' style in opposition to 'Pagan' classicism; he had in fact – forestalling Ruskin and Morris – seen style as a matter of morality rather than of taste.

With the seal of official approval set upon the Gothic of the Houses of Parliament we have barely arrived at the Queen's accession, but already, in that building, we can sense a forerunner of High Victorianism. It is not merely that the Palace of Westminster is official, or that it is large. It is also solid; it is expensive, it is patriotic, it is uninhibited, it is self-assured, it is highly organized and for liberal institutions. It may have been designed in the late thirties, but it is of the very essence of the Queen's reign.

There is a test for these things. Set the minor arts of the time against any building. It is an infallible test. In Palace Yard we cannot envisage, say, the chariots or the barouches of the Regency ... although these still existed when Barry was making his design. In the lobbies and vaulted corridors we cannot possibly envisage wigs or tricorn hats. It is the hansom-cabs, the toppers and the frock-coats that are all of a piece with the architecture. It is to their era, in spirit, if not in date, that the Houses of Parliament belong, not less than does the St Pancras Hotel thirty years later.

In the final phase of the Revival it remained only for Butterfield and Scott – although Gothic ran in their veins – to forget that Gothic had ever been part of the Middle Ages. That had become irrelevant. With their garish polychromy, their new shiny materials, their eclecticism and architectural arrogance, they gave us something new – a Victorian style, a 'modern' style. All Saints', Margaret Street (1849–59), the Albert Memorial (1864), the Law Courts (1871) and the St Pancras Hotel (1867), although we have dealt with them as part of the later Gothic Revival, are also among the principal monuments of High Victorianism.

It is the hardness and brashness, the uninhibited richness of mid-Victorian architecture that makes one know, somehow, that one has reached the heart of the age. The Victorian Age has been dismissed too often as an age of 'stylistic revivals'; it ultimately made these 'revivals' – whether Gothic or classic – so much an expression of itself that in the process they ceased to be revivals and became ... Victorian.

There is also evident in these buildings something the eighteenth century had never truly known. There is displayed in every brick a highly professional, but not artistic, expertise. The cultivated and dilletante English amateur has been replaced by the commercial practising architect – one can sense the office stools, the drawing-board, the draftsmen, the Academy perspective and the carefully drawn details which, so efficiently but so disastrously, had replaced the artist. That is the background of the architect of High Victorianism.

The vast prosperity of their time, the dozens of commissions all blazing ahead, as well as the efficient office in the background, all added to the self-assurance of the man, as well as to its expression in his work. Pugin's fanaticism was of a different order and may be forgiven; it was, like Butterfield's severity, born of his faith. Charles Barry's conceit, however, was inordinate; his insensitivity made him the mentor of an insensitive age; his ability to control and organize assured him a fine income. He was more than ready to rebuild half Whitehall, from the Mall to Birdcage Walk in the style of his own voluptuous Board of Works, and he nearly pulled it off.

As we look upon the Victorian architectural scene, it is difficult to decide which shows the greater self-esteem: the lightheartedness with which a Barry – like Wyatt before him or Norman Shaw after him – could switch from one style to another; or the absolute conviction with which a Street or a Scott could stock only Gothic goods – justifying themselves morally and losing nothing commercially.

Scott, for instance, although a businessman rather than a pietistic Gothic fanatic, could write:

The old and the new worlds were severed by the most marked line of separation which Providence had ever drawn between different periods of history – the destruction of the Roman Empire, and with it the arts and civilisation of the ancient world.

To ignore this dispensation was impious, and had resulted in the buildings of the 'vernacular classic style' with which he found himself surrounded. Of these, he states, 'I am just now hard at work, in more than one instance, in transforming their outside and their inside into my own style, and flatter myself that no one will ever regret the change.'

If the Victorian Age has been dismissed too often or too superficially as one of 'stylistic revivals' – without examining what that really means in terms of building – equally it has been said too often and too superficially that there was a 'collapse of taste'. Perhaps there was, but it would be much more to the point to say that there was a shift of patronage and a change of function. These things happen in history: in the sixteenth century there was a shift of patronage – from Church to Crown – and a change of function – from church to

69 John Nash: Cumberland Terrace

70 H. L. Elmes and C. R. Cockerell: St George's Hall

71 C. R. Cockerell: St George's Hall, Concert Hall

mansion ... whether that was a 'collapse of taste' has been a subject for argument ever since.

Although the Victorian aristocracy might, in a limited way, still patronize the arts, they no longer dictated taste. The real patrons were now the industrialists, magnates, brokers and so on, or – which came to much the same thing – Boards and City Councils composed of such men. They were not always the philistine upstarts they have been painted. They preferred the obvious to the subtle, the grand to the simple, ornament to proportion. Style and carving appealed to the intellect, elegance and harmony to the sensibilities ... and it was sensibility that was lacking. Wealth, self-assurance and romanticism could produce very good art or very bad. Perhaps that is why the individual architect, apart from his improved professional status, now seems to matter so much more than anonymous craftsmen.

That, also, is why the story of Victorian classic architecture is curiously parallel to that of the Gothic Revival. There was, first, the attenuated elegance of the late eighteenth century – no less an appendage of the Picturesque than Gothic. The hall-mark of, say, John Nash – whether we look for it on the Corinthian and Doric terraces of Regent's Park, or upon his battlemented castles, is unmistakable. There are Gothic interiors, Strawberry Hill, Stowe, Windsor and scores of others, quite palpably by the same band of plasterers as had created a thousand classic or Palladian drawing-rooms.

72 J. Young: Eaton Square, London. *In the Nash tradition in so far as it is specu-lative terrace housing with classical detail in stucco, but – compared with Nash – it gains in grandeur and loses in elegance. This may be just jerry-built snobbery but it is good 'townscape'.*

But, just as there was a moment – the building of the Houses of Parliament – when one suddenly knew that one really was within the Victorian era ... so with Classic. With Nash's white stucco terraces [69], with the neo-Grec of Inwood's St Pancras Church (1819) or the Bank of England (1788–1833) or Decimus Burton's Athenaeum (1827) one knows that this is still the Regency. In 1839, however, the young Harvey Lonsdale Elmes (1815–47) designed St George's Hall, Liverpool [70, 71]. This, like the Palace of Westminster, is a most magnificent monument to its age. Based upon the Thermae of Caracalla, set upon a stepped platform, and surrounded by a superb Corinthian peristyle, it is possessed of a true Roman *gravitas*. In that urban space, outside Lime Street Station, black with soot, it is also redolent of the great days of the industrial North. Once again, as at Westminster, one knows quite suddenly that the Queen reigns.

St George's Hall is not High Victorian, but it is the Classic forerunner, as Barry's building was the Gothic forerunner. A few years later Sir Robert Smirke (1780–1867) was completing the huge Ionic colonnades of the British Museum – less distinguished than St George's Hall, but with all the ponderous majesty and certainty that only Rome and Victorian England ever had [73]. In Liverpool and Bloomsbury, then, the age was fairly launched.

Once those almost eighteenth-century figures of Elmes, Smirke and Wilkins had left the stage, there remained only one man who could still show something of the fine scholarship of the Augustan Age – Charles Robert Cockerell (1788–1863). A sensitive and cultivated intellectual – the man who could read Lycophron at sight, could go further than Stuart in his observation of Hellenic refinements and could regard Sir William Chambers as his ideal, his mentor and as the 'last of the Romans', was clearly as far removed as could be from the realities of the century in which he lived. If architecture is merely a series of scholarly essays by great masters – scholarship itself being the deft handling of the architectural vocabulary of antiquity – then Cockerell must be judged the greatest of the lot. But of course architecture is much more than that. Cockerell's contribution to the life of his time, his influence upon that life and upon our life is precisely nil. The skill with which he could, say, model a pedimented attic storey above an engaged Roman Doric Order, was absolute! He was, above

74 C.R.Cockerell: Bank of England, Liverpool. *This beautifully designed classical façade shows how very skilfully Cockerell could handle the complexities of the Greek vocabulary when applying it to the sort of building for which it was never intended.*

75 Admiralty Arch and Trafalgar Square. *James Gibbs's church of St Martin-in-the-Fields still holds the corner of the Square at the highest point – otherwise Trafalgar Square is a typical Victorian mess that has just grown. Neither Wilkins's National Gallery, nor Aston Webb's vulgar Admiralty Arch, nor Herbert Baker's South Africa House, nor even Nelson, can give unity to a 'square' with nine streets coming into it.*

all things, an architects' architect, and he still is. He is best remembered, perhaps, for the very striking and 'intellectual' appearance of the Taylorian Institute in Oxford (1839). His Bank of England branch office in Liverpool (1845) is a perfect example of classic detail and surface modelling [74]. The small Concert Hall (1851) which he added to Elmes's St George's Hall was less successful because less restrained. His most glorious design (1839) was never built – it was for the Royal Exchange in London.

There were, in those Early Victorian years, a few other magnificent preliminaries to High Victorianism. There were, first, those two – Elmes's St George's Hall (1839) followed by Smirke's British Museum (1827–47). There was also William Wilkins's National Gallery (1838) not quite dominating Trafalgar Square, and famous mainly because it uses up the Corinthian columns from the old Carlton House. Wilkins was responsible for that beautifully restrained and composed campus at Downing College in Cambridge; also for a remarkable portico, high on a podium, at University College, London (1827). Then the Grecian seal was impressed upon the whole decade by Philip Hardwick's (1792–1870) Euston Propylaea [76].

76 Philip Hardwick: Euston Station, The Doric Propylaea

These buildings, as one might expect in face of both a rising romanticism and a rising industrialism, display their classicism rather ostentatiously. They might, it is true, veer between an expression of Roman weight and majesty – as exemplified at Liverpool – or a true Greek restraint as at Downing, but in those years the Classic Revival was far more archaeologically correct – for what that was worth – than had been either the picturesque elegance of Nash or the exquisite individualism of Soane a generation earlier. With such people as Pugin or Brunel on the warpath, the Classicists had to show the flag. Already that classical education and classical feeling that had been second nature to the Palladians could no longer be taken for granted. The snobbery that must actually demonstrate its knowledge of Greece and Rome was already present. The antique origins of architecture must be in no doubt. The ghost of the Caesars must haunt the colonnades of Smirke or Elmes, as surely as the ghosts of the Plantagenets must haunt the cloisters of Pugin. The engineers were philistines; the Gothicists were Bohemians; the Classicists were Correct ... that at least was their view [77, 78, 79].

All the works of the Early Victorian Classical Revival – large, dignified, restrained – show a very real comprehension and sensibility. With the new and crude sort of patronage, as well as with the more commercial architectural office, that sensibility faded. Without the passion, romance, piety or sheer afflatus that belonged to even the excesses of the Gothic Revival, High Victorian Classic – for all its considerable achievements – was usually pompous, over-ornamented, and alternatively either dull or vulgar.

In some ways, however, the parallel between the Gothic and the Classic story goes on into the middle years with such examples as Harrods or the Langham Hotel. The rich, colourful, bizarre 'modern' of Butterfield or Scott had its counterpart in a far less strictly correct 'classic' – a kind of mixed style, drawn from all over the place, and with only the use of the 'orders' to justify the word 'classic' at all.

Another ingredient of High Victorianism brings its architecture rather nearer to our own day. The more those buildings were distinctively Victorian, the less important seem the actual historical origins of their decorative detail – whether Classic or Gothic – and the more their historicism is in fact limited to mere detail.

77 Alexander Thomson: Caledonian Road Free Church, Glasgow. *A 'picturesque' handling of Greek elements showing that there is far more to Greek architecture than temple porticoes. A most skilful building.*

78 Thomas Hamilton: High School, Edinburgh. *This very beautiful composition is the architectural counterpart of the Athenian intellectualism that then reigned in Edinburgh.*

79 Alexander Thomson: Moray Place, Glasgow. *The Scottish genius for neo-Grec – product of Celtic romanticism and a classical education – applied to ordinary speculative terrace housing.*

That other ingredient may be described as 'organization'. This might seem to bring us towards our own functionalism, but while the word 'functionalism' has for us an aesthetic content – 'fitness for purpose' – 'organization' had ostensibly nothing to do with aesthetics. In fact of course it did dictate indirectly the whole form and massing of a building, but it was the ability of the architect to arrange or organize the plan of a complicated and extensive building that was the essence of the matter.

The seething, complex, technological Victorian Age demanded a host of buildings for hitherto undreamt of purposes. Railway stations and hotels replaced the old posting inn; huge docks and bonded warehouses replaced the harbour; flats – as we see them at Queen Anne's Mansions – were beginning to replace town houses and bachelors' chambers, culminating in the Arabian Nights fantasia of Whitehall Court. City halls, Assize Courts, hospitals, hotels [80, 81] were all different from their eighteenth-century counterparts, although the superficial difference in style has sometimes concealed the much greater difference in size and complexity. Museums, libraries, art schools were all part of that great cultural upsurge, that Victorian desire for enlightenment, that had grown out of the Romantic Movement; they were in fact its civic insignia.

If the new industrial cities, in those expanding years, built the slums, they also gave us some of the most extraordinary 'cultural' architecture in all history. St George's Hall, Liverpool, Waterhouse's Town Hall (1868) and Edward Walter's Free Trade Hall (1856), both in Manchester; Cuthbert Brodrick's black but festive Town Hall in Leeds [82], built in 1868, or, say, that curious and Corinthian 'Temple of Jupiter Stator' with which Joseph Hansom (inventor of the cab) provided Birmingham in 1846, were not mere town-halls; they were very large auditories for massed choirs, revivalist meetings and radical orators.

All these sorts of buildings needed highly organized plans, undreamt of in Georgian times. (Chambers's Somerset House, 1776, was the only Georgian building on a Victorian scale, while Soane's Courts for the Bank of England, in 1795, were the first tentative example of organized planning for commerce.) The Law Courts in the Strand had been the first really complicated problem in organizing a plan, and there, as we have seen, Street failed us. Barry, thirty years earlier, and before his time, had struck the true note with the tremendous efficiency of the Houses of Parliament – the various circulatory systems, royalty, peers, commons and public, are all beautifully clarified; every chamber and room is well-lit and quiet, and has its right place in a larger whole.

Perhaps, however, it is Alfred Waterhouse (1830–1905) who ranks as the High Victorian architect *par excellence*. Founder of a wealthy dynasty of architects and City men, Waterhouse cashed in on the golden age of the Manchester Philosophy – supply and demand, and devil take the hindmost. Waterhouse was artist enough to handle deftly his elaborate schemes of decoration, and yet philistine enough to handle these cotton merchants on their own terms ... in a city which seldom employed an architect twice. (Manchester is, for us, incidentally a museum piece with one example of the work of each eminent Victorian architect.)

Waterhouse's buildings, however, are not only monuments of the Gothic Revival; they are also examples of his power to organize diverse and complicated plans on a modern scale, if not in a modern style. That was something new in architecture – something that had not been needed since the Romans had had to handle the crowds of the Colosseum and the Thermae. It is the organization of space as opposed to mere façade.

Another aspect of High Victorianism is contained in the word 'Enlightenment'. It was the Early Victorian earnestness of Prince Albert that had inculcated those virtues of enlightenment and culture that were enshrined in the architecture of the next generation. It was Sherlock Holmes, as the train moved high on the embankment above South London, who pointed out to Watson those 'beacons of enlightenment' – the London Board Schools. They alone, with the Puseyite spires, broke the horizon above the grey ocean of Welsh slates.

Not till 1889 was the London County Council born out of a morass of vestries and pavement boards. It had a small architect's department – the first in the world – building the first municipal flats (Millbank, 1899 [86]) and the first municipal housing in 1903. The London School Board – duly absorbed in the L.C.C. – was economic but slightly Ruskinian in taste. It had built those 'beacons of enlightenment' that are, even today, too solid, too efficient and too well-lit to be

80 Cuthbert Brodrick: Grand Hotel, Scarborough. *The eighteenth century had many large hotels – mainly glorified posting inns. The real monsters – precursors of the Ritz, Savoy, etc. – did not originate, as is often supposed, in Paris or America, but in Victorian England. There was a clutch in Northumberland Avenue, and there were the big new resorts – the Metropole at Brighton or this huge affair at Scarborough.*

81 John Giles: Langham Hotel, Portland Place. *Another of the large hotels of the sixties – it was frequented by Ouida and is now part of the B.B.C. complex.*

82 Cuthbert Brodrick: The Town Hall, Leeds. *What a magnificent composition this is! In its coating of soot it is still both festive and dignified – an absolutely adequate expression of the mid-Victorian industrial city.*

83 W.Young: City Chambers, Glasgow. *If Leeds shows how good a Victorian town-hall could be, this one in Glasgow shows how bad. It lacks almost every real architectural quality.*

84 Alfred Waterhouse: Assize Court, Manchester

demolished. That was enlightenment on the rates. The enlightenment of High Victorian culture, however, could be more lavish in its planning, grotesque and fanciful in its ornament.

This is found not merely in the occasional town-hall or institute of the big provincial city: the Great Exhibition of 1851 had left behind it a large fund for a vaguely educational use. So, in South Kensington, between the Cromwell Road and Kensington Gardens – in what Mr Goodhart-Rendel has called 'the Brompton Art Quarter' – there lies the most astounding set of architectural specimens imaginable. Standing on some high tower in central London – ignoring the modern skyscrapers – the level line of trees and roofs is broken to the north by the pinnacles of St Pancras, to the south by the variegated towers of Kensington.

As town-planning this complex of buildings was disastrous – an axial plan with one building set behind another in a single line, southwards from the Albert Memorial for the best part of a mile [87]. Until

85 Alfred Waterhouse: The Town Hall, Manchester

the coming of air photography that long formal axis was invisible. An axis, the spine of all great planning in 'the high Roman manner', is something *around* which, not *along* which buildings may be arranged. But then it must be noted, as a characteristic of the age that there is an entire absence of town-planning everywhere. Whether as a manifestation of eighteenth-century order or of twentieth-century welfare, planning was a contradiction of Victorian individualism. Between the planning of Regent's Park in 1810 and the first Garden City in 1905, it was a dead art. South Kensington shows this very clearly indeed.

In sheer verve and architectural entertainment, however, the museums and colleges of South Kensington more than console us for the lack of planning. As early as 1855 Sir Henry Cole, prime mover in the matter on Albert's behalf, had had to house the collection of 'practical Art' already formed by the Government. He employed Sir William Cubitt, the engineer, to build the old Museum of Art and Science – soon to be known derisively as 'the Brompton Boilers'.

86 London County Council Architect's Department: Flats, Millbank, London.
*Just behind the Tate Gallery, this is a social as well as an architectural landmark.
Built by the newly founded L.C.C. this is probably the first housing in the world to be
built with public money. Its style would seem to confirm that the L.C.C. was advised
by W. R. Lethaby.*

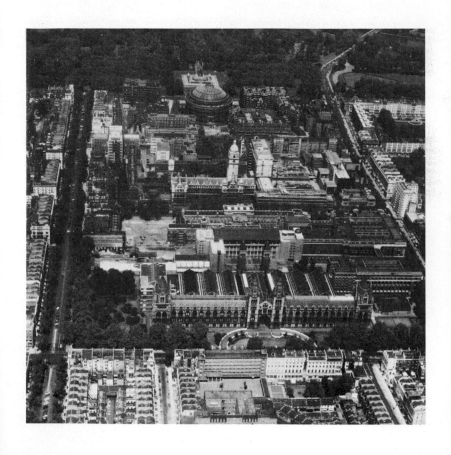

Real High Victorianism, however, did not burst upon South Kensington until 1879. At one end of that long axis the Gothic Revival had already implanted the Albert Memorial; at the other end Alfred Waterhouse now gave us his neo-Romanesque Natural History Museum – all in honey-coloured terra-cotta. That was the terra-cotta decade – a useful material, washable and cheaply moulded into ornament. It was being used elsewhere by Waterhouse, although in a kidney colour, at St Paul's School, Hammersmith and at the Prudential Insurance Office in Holborn, two buildings that are still easily discernible.

All the remaining buildings of the South Kensington group seem to have been infected by a certain Waterhouse richness, even if in date they are rather later. Waterhouse himself designed the City and Guilds College. Sir Aston Webb (1849–1930) was guilty of the Victoria and Albert Museum [88]. Sir Aston had a vast practice but he lacked Waterhouse's ability to organize a plan; the Victoria and Albert being designed as a place in which to get lost.

88 Francis Fowke: Victoria and Albert Museum, courtyard

89 H. Gribble: Brompton Oratory. *The 'old Catholics' – aristocratic families who managed to keep their religion at the Reformation – followed Pugin in his Gothic fanaticism; the Oxford converts – Newman, Faber, and the rest – wished to be more Italian than the Italians. Hence this piece of Baroque pastiche.*

The remainder of Sir Aston Webb's work belongs both in character and date either to that last phase of the reign – all jingoism, Kipling and Imperialism – or else to the even lusher, grosser years of the brief Edwardian interlude. The new façade of Buckingham Palace, with its gilded and sculptured gates and railings, the terra-cotta Law Courts and the University, both in Birmingham – the latter with an absurd Siena-like campanile, the Royal Naval College at Dartmouth and the Admiralty Arch, are only a few of the buildings that stemmed from this too prolific office. Aston Webb's Victoria Fountain, in front of Buckingham Palace, is a memorial that has deserved, but unaccountably escaped, the abuse poured upon the memorial of the Queen's husband.

To that same phase belongs the Imperial Institute, designed by T. E. Colcutt (1840–1924) in the year of the First Jubilee [90]. This is the finest of the South Kensington group. In spite of its unfortunate date, its colour – a white stone laced with bands of orange brick – was delicious; its skyline was no less enchanting. Now that it is being demolished it seems a mere concession to sentiment to preserve the central tower without also preserving all the attendant towers, turrets and minarets.

To refer here to these buildings, which belong to the turn of the century, is not out of place. Having nothing whatever to do with either the Arts and Crafts Movement or *Art Nouveau* – with which they were contemporary – they emerge as buildings of the Establishment, in fact and in spirit – each a Royal Academy set-piece of its year. As such they belong, in reality if not in actual date, to High Victorianism. As the Houses of Parliament and St George's Hall Liverpool, were forerunners of High Victorianism – so these fabulous works by men such as Aston Webb or Colcutt are the Indian summer of that style. Their self-assurance, their general air of vulgar richness, as well as their official status, all confirm this.

The very phrase 'High Victorian' would seem to imply a 'Victorian Style'. It would also seem to exclude such special things as: (a) buildings of iron and glass to which *we* attach importance as being part of the pre-history of our own architecture, but to which the Victorians themselves denied the very word 'architecture'. (b) The intensely religious efforts to achieve an authentic Gothic – the fanaticism of a

Catholic Pugin or an Anglican Butterfield was too rarified, too personal a thing to be regarded as the 'style' of an age. (c) The neo-Grec and all similar attempts – right on into this century – to revive historical styles in a literal way; clearly these cannot be a 'Victorian Style'. (d) The Morris-inspired attempt to recover a vernacular craftsmanship in building; however poetic the results, this could never be more than a protest *against* the age, never the style of the age itself.

The exclusion from our argument of all these things leaves us with the startling question – was there a Victorian style at all? The final answer will almost certainly be 'No'. The Victorian style might, at first, seem to be discoverable in the more sophisticated achievements of the Gothic Revival's public buildings ... but on analysis these prove to be a phase, the products of a decade rather than of a century. Secondly, the style might seem to be discoverable in that endless series of expensive buildings possessed of an uncanny genius for combining a maximum of ornament with a maximum of dullness. A stroll through the City of London, along Oxford Street or Bond Street or, indeed, through the centre of any great provincial city, demonstrates the architectural disaster of Victorianism ... inspiration, craftsmanship, patronage are all dead and gone. When the modern 'developer' or

91 View towards Ludgate Hill

92 Gilbert Scott: Foreign Office. *If the style was forced upon the architect, the general composition of towers and masses – as viewed from the bridge over the St James's Park Lake – is one of the more famous of London's fortuitously picturesque scenes.*

93 Highgate Cemetery. *Victorian funerary architecture, with all the vaults for the corpses of rich merchants and families, is a study in itself – easily undertaken by walking round the Highgate or the Brompton Cemeteries. It is somewhere at this point that we find it most difficult to get inside the Victorian mind.*

the bomber have done their worst it is this residue that must be looked upon as the essence of Victorianism. But that residue can hardly be called a 'style'. It has no consistency within itself. That residue – whether stone or brick or terra-cotta, whether classic, Gothic, Flemish, Genoese or Venetian – is just the multitude of buildings that no one any longer bothers to look at or to remember. There is no Victorian Style.

Fortunately the Victorian Age was so fast moving, so vital, so pregnant with ideas, that – although it may have failed as an age – it threw up an endless series of real innovators, geniuses and eccentrics; vulgar men, sure of themselves, of great energy and great originality.

The absence of a 'style' – a consistent and recognizable way of building – may differentiate the Victorian Age from those other periods of history that we associate with great architecture. This confirms the mysterious feeling that most of us, in any case, already have about the nineteenth century. The greatness of the Victorian Age is of a different kind from the greatness of other periods. That adds to rather than detracts from its fascination ... and that fascination is to be found as much in the age's architecture as in anything else.

Ruskin and Morris

In 1869 Henry James, having just dined with the Ruskins, wrote to his mother:

Ruskin himself is a very simple matter, In face, in manner, in talk, in mind, he is weakness pure and simple. He has the beauties of his defects . . . he has been scared back by the grim face of reality into the world of unreason and illusion. He wanders there without a compass and a guide – or any light save the fitful flashes of his beautiful genius.

To call Ruskin 'simple' must be counted one of Henry James's oddest perversities; that Ruskin had been scared by the grim face of reality was true. The consequences of that scared genius were of measureless import for Victorian England ... and, indirectly, for us.

All Ruskin is in his work. One must take him whole or not at all. And that is precisely what neither the Victorians nor we have ever done. The nineteenth century devoured his glowing and purple prose, and then – in his name – committed every kind of architectural vandalism. The twentieth century has ignored his teaching which – with its vast apparatus of Biblical allusion – it would not have understood anyway, has attributed to him opinions he never held, as well as buildings he never built – for he was not an architect. It has preferred the minutiae of his miserable marriage and heart-breaking love affairs. The sensitive child, who wept because the frost had touched the almond blossom, with a background that was all godliness, cleanliness, sweetness and good manners, became the supreme Victorian observer. His writing, always subjective, could be melancholy or moody, but it never dealt in speculation or abstraction. It was wholly concrete. True, it is all thought and feeling, but always thought and feeling through the eye.

John Ruskin came late in the Romantic Movement – he was born in 1819 – and from a host of earlier romantics he had inherited certain kinds of image, a certain kind of pantheism, a certain discerning eye. To these images, to this Wordsworthian vision of the world, he added his own ... and it was multifarious. A peasant woman walking like a princess, her child's mild eyes, the fritillaries in Christ Church Meadow, the discovery in *Anacreon* that the Greeks loved roses, snow crystals held up against the blue sky, the shapes of interlacing waves retreating on the shore, ivy and shells, the tall elms in Warwick Park, the tracery at Bourges, the St Mark's sculpture tossing like spray, or the whorls of seaweed in the lagoon tide ... and not least the artifacts of Man.

In his youth at Oxford, fired by the injustice being done to Turner and the Pre-Raphaelites, he wrote *Modern Painters*. Nominally a defence of Turner those five volumes were in fact a minute analysis of cloud forms, rocks, crystals, foliage and alpine peaks. Only later, after the first magic glimpse of Venice in 1841, do architecture and painting begin to outweigh Nature in his diaries. In spite of the Evangelical upbringing, in spite of Latin beggars, priests and fleas, in spite of the beauty of grey Northern spires, that was the moment when the South won his heart.

He is in Venice. 'Thank God I am here! It is the Paradise of cities ... I am happier than I shall ever be again.' Rome, impious and baroque, he left in gloom. But the marble, the water and the whole liquid shimmer of Venice, the baby crabs and the gondolas floating on the tide into the hall at Danieli's, could so easily make him forget all those anti-baroque, anti-pagan feelings so proper to a young Victorian. At Venice, Longhena's great church of Santa Maria della Salute is not the least of baroque monuments, but, standing as it does in glorious marine serenity between canal and lagoon, style is no longer relevant. St Peter's had been only 'a nice ballroom', but in Venice it was all different. 'On such a morning as this,' he could write – 'on such a morning as this the white Salute is enough to raise one from the gates of death.' And again, as he walks home in the evening: 'St Mark's was worth anything. The outlines of St Mark's ... with the last remains of day showing like moonlight under the arch, kept me fearless of air and water, and I believe scatheless.'

That was a cathartic as well as an ecstatic moment. It was a decisive moment in the story of Victorian architecture. The people of England never again looked upon architecture with quite the same eyes. Ruskin came back to his 'golden clasp upon the girdle of the earth', to the marble walls rising out of the salt sea. He saw Venice first as a 'temptation'; then came that 'luckless day' when, in the Scuola di San Rocco, he rediscovered for the world the power of Tintoretto. The golden choirs of Fra Angelico were forgotten. He was utterly crushed.

Tintoretto swept me away into the *Mare Maggiore* of the schools of painting which crowned the power and perished in the fall of Venice; so forcing me into the study of the history of Venice herself.

Modern Painters had interpreted Turner; now *The Stones of Venice* was to interpret Tintoretto. True, *Modern Painters* gave us the Alps, the clouds and the lamps of Heaven in the bargain; but then *The Stones of Venice* gave us the desolate poetry of the lagoons, and the whole genius of that city where Gothic and Byzantine meet.

So long as Ruskin's sensitivity could find itself in the Falls of Schaffhausen or the narcissus meadows at Vevay, then all was well. 'Nature', after all, could be almost synonymous with God the Father. But now, and it was very disturbing, he had looked upon the work of Papists long since dead, and found it good. He was leaving a safe, sweet world for a new kind of beauty – Catholic, sinister, cruel and, almost certainly, dirty. So he wore himself out, through three volumes, proving not only that the Renaissance was a manifestation of the Scarlet Woman, but that Gothic and Byzantine Venice – because she showed some little independence of the Papal States – was virtually Protestant. It was one of the silliest somersaults in all literature. The result was a great masterpiece.

In the chapter on St Mark's he makes the shattering statement that he had never known of a Christian 'whose heart was thoroughly set upon the world to come, who also cared about art at all'. He meant, of course, a Victorian Christian ... otherwise his statement would demolish those Medieval and Byzantine worlds that were his theme. But therein, also, lay the effectiveness of his appeal to a Victorian world; he was making a moral issue out of Mediterranean art. Standing within those golden caverns of St Mark's he bemoaned 'the lost

94 John Everett Millais: *John Ruskin. Painted in Perthshire, this was intended to be a portrait of Ruskin 'looking quietly downstream, upon a lovely piece of worn rock'. It was painted on a holiday when Millais was already in love with Ruskin's wife; also at a time when Ruskin was deep in* The Stones of Venice *and thus revolutionizing the English attitude to architecture.*

power of Byzantine domes over the human heart', and there experienced his first doubts about his mother's Bible teaching. In his autobiographical *Praeterita* he denied that he could ever have become a Catholic – although for years Manning expected it – but that loss of faith, of which his readers never knew, was a partial victory over Protestant England by the ghosts of dead Venetian doges.

The clue to his real purpose, however, is a passage of Evangelical temper when he says that 'so long as our streets are walled with barren brick' or our faculties starved of beauty, it may be positively harmful to delight the senses just when they should be composed for devotion. There, for a second, it is Sunday morning in a bare Camberwell chapel, but the key phrase is: 'so long as our streets are walled with barren brick'.

The whole point about those golden caverns of St Mark's is that they were not for starved faculties and were not unique; they were merely the shrine of a whole golden city. And even Venice had not been unique among cities ... unique now because her lagoons have isolated and protected her; once the whole Gothic world was studded with such jewels. Even London, the London of Richard II was not less fair. The mutilated cathedrals only misrepresent that world, for in it they were merely incidents, nodal points as it were, in cities and landscapes of the same fabric as themselves.

Thus, while admitting that the loveliness of Venice and the power of Tintoretto were the temptation that led him on, it was with a social conscience to match his sensitivity that Ruskin wrote *The Stones of Venice*. It was all a sacrifice and a duty in the high, moral Victorian manner. Architecture, thereafter, ceased to be a matter of taste, it became a matter of morality. (It still is; all the controversies of this century – should one copy old styles, should form follow function and so on – have all been seen not as matters of taste but as matters of right and wrong.)

The first sentence of *The Stones of Venice* makes it all quite clear. Ruskin compares the three thrones set upon the sand: Tyre, of which only the memory remains; Venice, of which only the ruin; and London, which if she forgets the example of the others, 'may come to less pitied destruction'.

Ruskin may have written a good deal of nonsense about the morality and piety of the workman; never analysing the fundamental plan or structure of buildings, but reading far too much into ornament; into whether or not, for example, a carved flower is turned to the sun. But it was in Venice that he took the step that great artists have to take, from intrinsic beauty to social passion, ethics and political economy. The central work of his life was that chapter in the second volume of *The Stones of Venice* called 'The Nature of Gothic'.

Just as Ruskin never allowed the beauty of Catholic art to turn him into a Catholic, so he never allowed his belief in the happiness and piety of the Medieval workman to turn him into a Socialist. In *Unto This Last* (1860), he came very near to it, as he had already done in 'The Nature of Gothic'. The true nature of Gothic, he says, is

the dependence of all human work for its beauty, on the happy life of the workman . . . you must either make a tool of the creature, oₐ a man of him. You cannot make both.

The modern trade union is not the medieval guild – and it is absurd to pretend that it is – but great art cannot be produced by unhappy men. All that – in a smug world of academicians, patrons and industrial bosses – was shattering. That chapter was reprinted as a penny pamphlet for working-men, and again by William Morris's Kelmscott Press, Morris saying that it was 'one of the very few necessary and inevitable utterances of the century'.

'The Nature of Gothic' was the strongest link in the chain that bound Morris to Medievalism, also in the chain that bound him to Socialism. If, at the time, all this seemed only another phase in the tale of the Gothic Revival, ultimately the equation ran: Medievalism plus Socialism equalled Craftsmanship; and Craftsmanship purged of its Medievalism equalled Functionalism. We still live within a continuation of the story.

If Ruskin's statement about the sort of art that produced Medieval labour made Morris a Socialist, then, equally, the statement about the sort of labour that produced Medieval art, confirmed Morris in all his 'Gothic opinions'. Not the least part of 'The Nature of Gothic' was Ruskin's famous defence of the North against the South, his distinction 'between the district of the gentian and the olive which the stork and the swallow see far off, as they lean upon the sirocco wind': – or

– for all his love of Venice – his contrast between the parapets of St Mark's rearing themselves like spray against the blue sky, and the rooks cawing around Salisbury spire on a grey morning. That was, for Morris, another decisive moment, the proof that northern towers and buttresses were not just an eccentric taste, but one of the world's great architectures, and above all that that architecture was not a mere way of building, but part of a way of life.

William Morris (1837–96) was seventeen years younger than Ruskin, whom he always called his 'master'. He was not an architect; his influence upon architecture was profound. Professor Pevsner's classic work, *Pioneers of the Modern Movement* (1936) bore the sub-title, 'From William Morris to Walter Gropius'. That gives authority to the significance of Morris; it suggests, however, that the generation from Morris to Gropius was a self-contained historical sequence. In fact Morris came not at the beginning of a story, but in the middle. He carried architectural thought from the stylism of the Gothic Revival into the opening phases of the Modern Movement.

That Modern Movement owes much to Morris, but Morris, although he wore his Gothic with a difference, was really a figure of the Gothic Revival. More than Pugin – who adored Gothic for theological reasons, more than Butterfield or Street – who used it for professional ends; more even than Ruskin – whose Anglican insularity blinded him to some aspects of the Middle Ages ... more than any of these Morris had the clear vision of a dreaming romantic. It was Morris whom Yeats had in mind when he wrote:

> We were the last romantics – chose for theme
> Traditional sanctity and loveliness.

And yet, more than any of the others, did Morris look with wide open eyes upon the horrific sight of Victorian England. He applied – and effectively – romantic thinking to real life.

It is usual to emphasize Morris's versatility – painter, weaver, dyer, glazier, typographer, poet, merchant, socialist. On the face of it this versatility would seem to put Morris with the great masters of the Renaissance. Versatility, however, is not in itself a merit. A man's greatness does not lie in doing a number of things – that may be only a dissipation of energy – but in the singleness of vision of which they are the parts. Morris's works are so often enumerated without study, or studied in isolation, that it is worth glancing at the whole to discover why he is a significant figure, to discover some unity of vision which may explain both the Kelmscott Press and the wallpapers, the Red House and *The Defence of Guenevere*, the Socialist League and the firm of Morris & Co.

The unity underlying Morris's activities is to be found mainly in Yeats's lines, in the whole of Morris's vast inheritance from the Romantic Movement; it is also to be found in his own integrity, or, to paraphrase the title of half-a-dozen books – 'Morris, Romantic and Revolutionary'. He is the link between the Gothic Revival and Karl Marx.

Morris was on the side of the master-carver of Chartres, looking out over the fields of waving corn; he was on the side of the Guild of Ghent in their revolt against the Count of Flanders – triumph of craftsman over feudalism – and he was, as he said, 'on the side of Karl Marx *contra mundum*'. Trade Unionism, the Welfare State and, above all, new industrial techniques, have created a society and an architecture very far from *The Dream of John Bull* or *News from Nowhere*, and as joyless, if cleaner, in its work as was ever the nineteenth century. But Morris must still be looked upon as one of our founding fathers, even if he is the one we have betrayed. He would still see our civilization as doomed, but would still console himself – as he wrote in 1885 – with the thought of 'barbarism once more flooding the world'.

In 1853 Morris came to an Oxford still fantastically Medieval, rural and Tractarian. His state of mind was one of sickening horror against the economic system – a horror first sparked off by the mass-produced objects shown in the Great Exhibition of 1851. This horror arose not only from the objects themselves – their irrationality, over-ornamentation and general idiocy; it arose from the whole nature of an industrial era, from the whole cash-nexus which could not only make such things possible, but could be proud of them. Above all, that horror was inspired by the cruelty, the misery, the ugliness and human degradation which industrialism implied and, indeed, seemed to necessitate. Against that degradation of Man, Morris set his dream of the Middle Ages. He then spent the rest of his life trying to put things right.

In Morris's complex existence there was more than one decisive moment. One, certainly, was his reading of Carlyle's *Past and Present* in 1865. Three years earlier Carlyle had spoken of Ruskin's *Unto This Last* as having effectively 'blown up the world that calls itself "Art"'. *Past and Present* is now a half-forgotten but once almost seminal book. Although it dealt not at all with architecture, it did confirm Morris in his view of Medieval life. Carlyle's analysis of the well-ordered and benign life of the Abbey of St Edmund, under the good Abbot Sampson, was – like Pugin's *Contrasts* – a shock to Victorian complacency. It revealed the Middle Ages, not as some myth of warring knights; it revealed them as being not only picturesque, but also wise, not only pious but also civilized. The wisdom of Greece and Rome had not, after all, been buried pending a Renaissance awakening, but had been stored in every Benedictine library, where Aristotle was second only to Christ.

Morris, having married, was determined to build himself a house and to make the furniture for it. Although never an architect, he had served for a time in the Oxford office of George Edmund Street, and there met Philip Webb (1831–1915). This friendship was a fruitful one. Taken in conjunction with the start of the firm of Morris, Marshall, Falkner & Co., in 1861, it may be said to have been the foundation of the Arts and Crafts Movement, with all that that implies ... Morris's own textiles and wallpapers, the furniture of people like Ernest Gimson or Ambrose Heal, the whole revival of the English vernacular as we see it in the work of Voysey, Webb or the young Lutyens. It became a European movement, culminating in 1905 in the publication of Muthesius's monumental *Das Englisch Haus*. Its swan song, perhaps, may be seen in the lovely Gothic craftsmanship of Ninian Comper (1861–1961), or the interiors of Ostberg's Town Hall at Stockholm.

In the end it all had to be transmuted, mainly by Walter Gropius, in terms of the Bauhaus, the machine and the twentieth century. Those terms, those products of the mechanized workshop, appropriate for an architecture of glass and steel, were something which Morris would have violently repudiated. Nevertheless, since they involved the process of design, they could never have come into being without him ... or without the Red House – the home which Philip Webb built for him in 1859 [95].

95 Philip Webb: The Red House. *The famous house that Webb built for the young William Morris – a quite genuine revival of the English vernacular and of craftsmanship in building. It was a revolutionary building at that date ... it led straight to Norman Shaw, Voysey and Lutyens.*

The Red House at Upton, although now devoured by the suburban sprawl of south London, still stands in its old apple orchard. At the time it did not attract much attention; it now appears in every text-book as a 'landmark' in the history of the English house. It was certainly a landmark in the story of Morris's influence upon architecture.

The most significant thing about the Red House was not how Gothic it was – one or two pointed arches, no more – but how un-Gothic. A generation had gone by since Pugin had built the Lancashire mansion of Scarisbrick, a house rich in ecclesiastical Gothic detail – the whole apparatus of pinnacle, mullion and tracery, such as no medieval house had ever known. Since then, mainly in the wealthier suburbs of the big cities the influence of a much misunderstood Ruskin had also given us the Venetian mansions of rich magnates or the Gothic villas of the middle class.

It was the infinite good fortune of Morris's generation to 'discover' the English Cotswolds – quiet and forgotten glory of an older England. The effect was tremendous. The medieval craftsman, it was now seen, did not work only upon St Mark's or Amiens or Wells; he might very likely be found in the next village. The Red House was a reflection of this discovery.

It was not a wholly successful design although the best Philip Webb ever did. He became too much an eclectic stylist. In the Red House, however, the stylistic trappings are absent. There is a self-conscious touch here and there, as in the high turreted French roof or the whimsical well-head, but in 1859 the design was astonishing for its simplicity. Other houses were either full-blooded Ruskinian Gothic or, even into the sixties, classic stucco. As the name of Morris's house implies, the use of naked red brick and tile was a gesture of defiance. It was to be another generation before Dutch bricks and hand-made tiles would be available, but at least it was now recognized that a plain brick wall might be just as much a piece of craftsmanship as an oak dresser or a De Morgan plate.

That was a momentous step. As Morris's dye works at Merton, his stained glass, or the Kelmscott Press each gave new life to some ancient craft, so did the Red House bring back into architecture sound building and a respect for the vernacular. With its basically simple

96 William Morris: 'Compton' chintz

forms, its tall chimney stacks and long ridge lines, the Red House made form more important than ornament. It also opened the way for such fashionable domestic architecture as that of Norman Shaw (1831–1912) or Edwin Lutyens (1869–1944), as well as for such things as the cult of the week-end cottage, and its ultimate degradation in spec' housing and the 'stockbrokers' Tudor' of the prosperous suburbs.

In their emphasis upon basic form, upon good material, upon design and workmanship, Morris and Webb were on the verge of a discovery – that orthodox Gothic forms are almost the least part of the Gothic style [97]. With his organ cases, his stained glass and his typography, Morris played the Gothic game to the end, but in that short partnership with Philip Webb, he produced something that was independent, not of course of all medieval feeling – that would be asking too much – but certainly of all specifically Gothic ornament. This was a house that Pugin would have disliked, and which Frank

97 William Morris: The settle at the Red House

Lloyd Wright loved. It bridges the century from the 'Gothick' of Wyatt to the organic architecture of Lloyd Wright. That, rather than its intrinsic merit, has made it a landmark.

Wherein, then, lay Morris's failure? He knew that great architecture was born of the consummated marriage of Man and Nature. He knew, perhaps too well, that the Middle Ages were one of those rare moments in history when that consummation had taken place. What he failed to realize was that that moment could never be re-created. Pugin thought that by pointing to the beauties of Gothic he could bring lost souls into the arms of the Church; Morris thought that by pointing to the happiness of the Middle Ages, he could persuade Industrialism to abolish itself. That, however, was not to be had for the asking. Morris should have known better; you may condemn, you may even alter things just a little; you can never put history into reverse.

Morris [writes Professor Pevsner], looks backward, not forward, into the times of the Icelandic Sagas, of Cathedral building, of Craft Guilds. One cannot, from his lectures, obtain a clear view of what he imagined the future to be.

That is true ... Morris had no such view.

All the same Morris was right, Gropius wrong. Men can only be happy working with their hands. But Morris should have realized that

98 Philip Webb: Clouds, drawing-room. *Lovely as this room is – as an example of Webb's later work – it also shows how much more sophisticated and 'stylish' he had become since the first pristine days of the Red House.*

his intellectual Ludditism was a kicking against the pricks. The machine is with us. It was already there in Morris's day. It may be hated with some reason, but it must be used and exploited, not repudiated. That, in due course, was to be Gropius's contribution – to design *for* the machine, not against it. When the young Morris, in 1851, saw the objects in the Crystal Palace, his nausea was a perfectly correct reaction. Those objects were the product of machines wrongly used. What Morris failed to see was that up there above his head in the Crystal Palace, in the iron and the glass, was a new architecture.

It is all summed up in two famous statements. 'Art,' said Morris, 'will die out of civilization, if the system lasts. That in itself does to me carry with it a condemnation of the whole system.' The reply, almost a challenge, came years later when Frank Lloyd Wright, in 1901, read his manifesto on *The Art and Craft of the Machine*. Looking out upon the towers and lights of Chicago by night, he said: 'If this power must be uprooted that civilisation may live, then civilisation is already doomed.'

8

Arts and Crafts, and Art Nouveau

Full-blooded High Victorian architecture – expensive, ornamental, uninhibited, stinking of the drawing-board and the office stool – was with us into this century. Like all large, rich styles – like Baroque or the Elizabethan mansions – it flattered its builders, or rather it flattered their institutions – the Academy, the Classes, the City. In a diluted form it is still with us; wherever there is pomposity there will be a pompous architecture.

However, once we are well into the second half of the nineteenth century; once *Past and Present, The Stones of Venice, Unto This Last* and *News from Nowhere* had been well and truly absorbed into the nation's blood-stream, there was – at least in progressive quarters – a change of climate, subtle but unmistakable. 'Taste', 'richness', 'style' give way to moral issues – the right and wrong way to build. The old issue of one style versus another still goes on, but another burning issue is whether or not there should be a 'modern' style – a style of iron and glass; yet another issue is contained in the question, 'What is an architect? Is he a gentleman or a craftsman?'.

Throughout the century the architect was much concerned to increase his professional status ... after all many Victorian architects were only one remove from the builder's yard. Morris, however, had emphasized that there are at least some things in good building which cannot be drawn, that can only be done by common working men, with their hands. Perhaps, after all, the most significant thing of all about the Red House was that it was carefully designed upon the drawing-board, by Philip Webb, to look as if it had not been designed upon the drawing-board at all. Significantly, in 1891 when the RIBA was promoting a Registration Bill in Parliament, a group of artists – including Alma-Tadema, Burne-Jones, Walter Crane, Holman Hunt and William Morris, non-architects caring more about art than status

– published an emphatic protest entitled, *Architecture: a Profession or an Art*. The issue was real. If there were to be examinations, for instance, what would be the fate of the 'Gothic' student faced by a 'Classical' examiner? Had any of the great architectures of the world ever been born on the drawing-board? Since Brunelleschi and Alberti, in fifteenth-century Florence, had started a process which had ended in the death of the craftsman throughout Europe, the issues argued by these Victorian architects had in fact been very real indeed. The elegant taste of the eighteenth century had masked the crisis; the collapse of that taste and the wider or more democratic use of architecture, had made it more acute.

But [as Mr Frank Jenkins has written in his essay, *The Victorian Architectural Profession* (1963)], the dreams of the Romantic artist – or even of William Morris's honest craftsman – were transitory; ultimately the facts had to be accepted as they existed. Pugin's New Jerusalem could not be reconciled with Victorian material progress, with the mill and the mine, the factory and the counting-house. It was the age of the 'man of affairs', and eventually the champions of the closed profession won the day. Statutory registration of architects was finally achieved by the Act of 1938; nevertheless it was a Victorian victory rather than a twentieth-century one, for by the end of Victoria's reign the battle was virtually over.

So, in the latter years of the century, we have an extraordinary situation. The majority of architects still waged the arid 'battle of the styles' and were concerned mainly with their own prosperity and social position. There was an enlightened minority – some of whom saw hope of a new architecture in the kind of building that was not designed by architects at all, but by engineers. Others saw the salvation of architecture in some kind of revival of an old vernacular such as had existed in, say, the fourteenth century, but again had never been in the hands of architects – only of master masons and country builders.

We have, then, four interwoven movements. One: the conservative and established architects designing in the recognized styles, mainly for conservative and philistine patrons. Two: the first stirrings of a consciously functional architecture, using engineers' ideas and materials – iron and plate glass. Three: the architects who, inspired by Morris, formed the Arts and Crafts Movement, reviving the English vernacular, using traditional materials and craftsmen in a medieval manner – in so far as this was possible – but eschewing the more obvious forms of medieval ornament – for which, in any case, the craftsmen were not available. This craft movement is really just one more phase of the Gothic Revival, even if its lack of ornament and workmanlike simplicity has sometimes made it seem like the beginnings of functionalism. Four: the conscious escape from all historicism of any kind, combined, however, with a refusal to abandon ornament as such; this meant the use of 'invented' ornament – the swirling lines and strangely bizarre shapes of *Art Nouveau*.

The first of these four – the well-established architects working in one of the two recognized styles – Classic or Gothic – meant little more than the continuation of High Victorianism into Edwardian times ... virtually the story of Gilbert Scott to Aston Webb. It is a story that had its achievements on its own dubious terms; it ended in the comic tragedy of reducing architecture to a formula – 'Classic for banks, Gothic for churches' ... many architects being willing to do either, on demand.

The second of these movements – the use of iron and glass in an 'architectural' as opposed to a 'utilitarian' manner, by architects as well as by engineers, had become inevitable after the success of Bunning's highly ornamental cast-iron Coal Exchanges in 1849 and, above all, after the success of the Crystal Palace in 1851. We have seen (p. 135) how these signal successes, followed by the Gothically enriched cast-iron roof of the Oxford Museum in 1855, or Boileau's iron Gothic church in Paris (1854) had caused Gilbert Scott in 1858, Viollet-le-Duc in 1870 – and even Ruskin – to admit grudgingly that the use of iron must lead to new architectural laws. Those laws, however, came only at the end of the century and, significantly, in the new and raw and uncultured city of Chicago. They belong not here, but (Chapter 10) to the birth of modernity.

The Arts and Crafts movement was to some extent – like Pre-Raphaelitism or Impressionism – a left-wing and Bohemian affair. In its attitude to the honest workman – idealized as an artist – it was bound to have links with Morris's socialism; in its utter repudiation of all the established vulgarity of the age, it was inevitably Bohemian. That it has also been associated with homespun tweeds and blue linen shirts, with ale and guilds, with the simple life and – ultimately – with the 'villagey' pattern of the Garden Cities, has also been inevitable. Morris's versatility – poetry, printing, textiles, furniture, pottery and so on – involved his disciples not only in a particular kind of art, but a particular way of life.

Like all such movements, it had its foolish side as well as its very real achievements. The passionate romanticism of its adherents, as well as the hideous transformation of England under their eyes, gave them a high conviction whereby they could take their theories to a logical conclusion. If Philip Webb, through the drawing-board, had, in the Red House, given us the simulacrum of a craftsman-built house from the days when there were no drawing-boards, it remained for Ernest Gimson (1864–1920) to gather together a group of under-graduates and set them to work with their own hands – and no draw-ings – building cottages in Charnwood Forest in Leicestershire [99].

99 Ernest Gimson: Lea Cottage

If the idea seemed extreme at the time, it must be remembered that it was, among other things, a protest against the state of building. Those cottages have thick stone walls and thatched roofs; they have 'medieval' plans, ingles, bread ovens and newel stairs. They are highly bucolic, but of course in the last analysis their extreme simplicity is only a disguise for an extreme sophistication. (There again lies the inevitable falsity of any revival, even of an unsophisticated style.) The cottages, however, are an architectural match for Gimson's furniture ... and did not Professor Pevsner call Gimson 'the greatest of the English artist-craftsmen'? Gimson's chairs and cabinets have a superb simplicity that is, in furniture, somehow less bogus than it is in the cottages [100,101]. This was the kind of furniture that was first sold by Ambrose Heal. Heal's shop was the first to break with the Victorianism of the Tottenham Court Road, and for a generation upheld a fine craft tradition.

If Gimson's 'hand-built' cottages strike a false note, it is only because they carry Morris's teachings to a logical conclusion in a world where those teachings are a contradiction in terms. What the Arts and Crafts movement did was to bring about a vastly increased respect for the English village, to open people's eyes to the beauty and fine qualities of old cottages, farms, barns and the simpler manor houses. Now that these things are an objective for any afternoon's motor ride, now that the 'beamed' week-end cottage and 'ye olde' tea-shop are a commonplace, it is as well to remember that a respect for the fine English vernacular is barely a hundred years old. It was not till 1877 that Morris founded the Society for the Protection of Ancient Buildings, a landmark in the movement ... and still important.

C.F.A. Voysey (1857–1941) is a central figure. In his respect for craftsmanship and tradition, in his versatility in designing textiles, furniture, silverware and wallpapers, as well as buildings, he is in the true Morris line. In an occasional flourish or twirl of his ironwork, an occasional attenuated chair or newel, he is on the flank of *Art Nouveau*. In his love of the unadorned surface, in his horizontal fenestration and long low lines, as well as his insistence upon fitness for purpose, he has been claimed as a 'pioneer of the modern movement', although in fact he lived long enough to hate almost all modern architecture. He was a professional architect, practising no craft

100 Ernest Gimson: Dining-room chairs

himself but gaining his ends, almost miraculously, as did Philip Webb, through the drawing-board.

Voysey's houses of the nineties – best among them are Perrycroft on the Malvern Hills (1893) and Broadleys on Lake Windermere (1898) – while looking back in some ways to the Red House, also inspired a whole generation of country-house architecture [103]. At its best that architecture is found in the excessively picturesque work of Baillie Scott (1865–1945) or in the dream-like country houses of the young Lutyens (1869–1944), built mainly for the aesthetic rich of the Edwardian era. At its worst the 'Voysey tradition' degenerated into sham suburban Tudor or the whimsies of the spec' builder. It was an architecture so dependent upon integrity of materials and design that it was all too easily debased. The note common to the houses of the Voysey–Lutyens era is the high gabled roof with its long ridge lines and big chimney stacks, the cottage window – stone or oak mullioned

101 Ernest Gimson: A chest

– and the general masking of internal upper-class comfort by an external cottage cosiness ... all very false but very charming.

Voysey's work had an astonishing freshness in an age that was still stuffy [104]. The interior of his own house – The Orchard, Chorley Wood, Buckinghamshire – has much white-painted woodwork, intense blue tiles to the fireplace, furniture of unpolished and unstained oak ... all novelties seventy years ago. The same is true of his textiles and wallpapers. He was here, in fact, much nearer to Nature than even Morris had been, also perhaps nearer to decorative charm ... although never allowing his kindly love of Nature to destroy the necessary formality of a textile design. As Van der Velde, the veteran Belgian architect, said of Voysey's wallpapers: 'It was as if Spring had come all of a sudden.'

There was at the time, and still is, much confusion between the Arts and Crafts movement in England, and that wider international

102 Ernest Gimson: The White House

fashion – *Art Nouveau*. At least two books, one German, one French – *Das Englisch Haus* (1905) by Hermann Muthesius, and *L'Architecture Moderne en Angleterre* (1890) by Paul Sédille – were richly illustrated and analysed the work that had been going on in England. Voysey, deservedly, and Baillie Scott, more dubiously, acquired great international reputations ... to some extent for the wrong reasons. Divorced as they were, in German and French minds, from the reformist and socially conscious teaching of Ruskin and Morris, they were misunderstood. Voysey might here and there give an irrational twist to a baluster or a railing ... to dub him, in consequence, an *Art Nouveau* architect was absurd. He was concerned with the reform of building, with eradicating ornament from the whole system, not with adding it.

Art Nouveau is seen now mainly as a fashion derived from Belgium and from France. In Brussels Victor Horta (1861–1947), through exploiting the plasticity of concrete and the ductility of steel, had made an architecture of swirling lines and undisciplined motifs ... the kind of thing that Van der Velde, in his lectures of 1894 and 1900, referred to as the kind of ornament which can express 'by means of pure structure ... joy, lassitude, protection, etc.'. In France it was the engineers such as Gustave Eiffel (1832–1923) who had shown that the liberation of form might arise from the use of metal. This had nothing

103 C.F.A. Voysey: House at Shackleford. *One sees here the curiously ambivalent position of Voysey. In the 'functional' square mullions and general austerity of detail, one can just see why he is considered a pioneer of modernism, but to build a gabled house with tall chimneys and mullioned windows of any kind shows where his heart was.*

104 C.F.A. Voysey: The Homestead. *This interior shows some of the very few touches of* Art Nouveau *detail that Voysey allowed himself. The full-blooded ornament of the Belgian Horta or of Mackintosh would have been contrary to the puritan severity of Voysey's temperament.*

105 Bruce Talbert: Design for an interior. *This drawing for a 'modern' interior, from* The Studio, *may stir memories for older readers. It is an amalgam of most of the current 'gimmicks' and was intended, no doubt, to appeal to* avant-garde *Chelsea.*

106 Walton: The Leys, billiard room. *A good example of a fine room – plus every possible* Art Nouveau *ornament and detail. Note, for instance, the light fittings, balusters, billiard-table legs, beaten copper and so on.*

to do with the great structural potentialities of steel; there were a number of buildings – Eiffel's Pavilion in the Paris Exhibition of 1878, and his Tower of 1889, as well as several highly ornate glass and metal Parisian department stores, which showed the possibilities of this *Art Nouveau.*

These buildings would have been as violently repudiated by Voysey as they would have been by Morris. They may explain the English use of a French name for a style that the French called simply 'modern', the Germans '*Jugendstil*' and the Italians – punning upon the name of the London shop – '*stile* Liberty'. In fact, considered over the whole field of *fin-de-siècle* art – literature, painting, typography, architecture – the explanation of *Art Nouveau* is more profound than the architectural historians have admitted, also more English. That explanation is psychological, social and sexual; it is found deep in the inherent contradictions of Victorian England. It was never openly obscene – apart perhaps from the subtle and latent evil of a Beardsley drawing – nor even, by Victorian standards, improper. It was, nevertheless, a revulsion against those standards and, as such, continually suspect.

The pendulum was swinging again. As the Gothic Revival had been a reaction against the aristocratic classicism of the eighteenth century, so now, after a hundred years of *bourgeois* morality, *Art Nouveau* was an expression of a new mood … on the frivolous plane it was the 'naughty nineties' and *épater les bourgeois*; on a more serious plane it was the hedonism of Swinburne or Wilde, or the new morality of Ibsen and Shaw.

There was certainly nothing suspect about, say, the posters of the Beggarstaff Brothers, the Gibson Girl, about Mackintosh's attenuated furniture or even Whistler's Peacock Room. But they are symptoms, and we may perhaps set in symbolic opposition to each other the young phthisic sensual Beardsley and the elderly, celibate and pietistic Butterfield, or the gay, mischievous art-for-art's-sake Whistler and the strict structural integrity of Voysey. That they are all Victorians gives the measure of the change now taking place, as well as of the complexity of the age.

If *Art Nouveau* can now be seen as a kind of interlude, it was not an irrelevant one in the story of art, not even in the practical art of architecture. It weaves itself into our larger tapestry. Romanticism, being the divine discontent of the artist, is also his flight from reality to dream worlds. One aspect of the story, therefore, is bound to be the artist's discovery of exoticism. Architectural theory in the nineteenth century has so far been explicable in terms of theology, morality or structure. Although tempered by the perpetual impact of Imagination, it has been a puritanical story. But architecture, being an art, cannot be thus limited indefinitely. If one kind of sensual pleasure – historical ornament – is rejected, then some other will take its place.

In architecture *Art Nouveau* did not even have to await its more obvious manifestations as we find them in Wilde, Beardsley and 'the Yellow Book' – that short-lived journal which gave its name to an epoch. The most obvious form of this exoticism – one from which its more architectural forms are derived – is the *Femme Fatale*. The *Femme Fatale* is a Harpy, a Medusa, she is Medea. Then, in our time, she is Wilde's Salomé, or she is there in Beardsley's Erda, or indeed in almost every woman he ever drew. She is, above all, Swinburne's Dolores, the Lady of Pain. At the height of Victorian puritanism, the *Femme Fatale* had already appeared. She had been taken out of myth and out of history by the Pre-Raphaelites ... mainly by Rossetti, the only visionary and voluptuary of the Pre-Raphaelite movement. For Rossetti she was the Beata Beatrix; she was Lynette or Elaine; she was *La Belle Dame sans Merci*. Sometimes she was Gothic, sometimes ghostly or attenuated. Like *Art Nouveau* architecture she was romanticism stripped of historic form. In real life she was Jane Morris or Lizzie Siddal – goitrous, heavy-lidded, green-eyed. In other guises she was the woman of those odd decorative panels – the Monna Vanna or the Sibylla Palmifera – that Rossetti has left scattered through our provincial galleries.

Now this *Femme Fatale*, whether of the sixties or the nineties, so haunted the Victorian scene as to become a type, and to demand a setting. And that setting, clearly, could never be anything so specific as Gothic. It could be an enchanted forest; it could be a dream; it was sometimes a meadow of passion flowers, or tall lilies in a fair garden. In architecture that setting became progressively less real, less stylistic, more abstract – the painter's attenuated lilies, transmuted into ornament, tended to become long stalks with little buds, until attenuation and swooning curves were all that was left. Those swooning curves, however, need not be limited to the pages of 'The Yellow Book', nor even to wrought iron or beaten copper. They could be painted panels, they could be stained glass, they could be wallpaper. They could be steel – for steel is ductile and can be curved, drawn out and shaped. The work of Horta in Brussels, of Sullivan in Chicago, and of Mackintosh in Glasgow can be explained in these terms.

Art Nouveau, because it was meant to express a passion, was no less a modern style. Like the functionalism that followed it, it repudiated historical ornament, but believed profoundly in ornament of some kind. (Remember that all Victorians lived in the shadow of the idea that 'ornamented building' was a definition of architecture.) You might oust the Gothic cusps and foliations, but the vacuum must be filled. In effect, if you got rid of one kind of ornament – the historical – you had to invent another – the exotic. Thus, rather surprisingly, we find the more precious *fin-de-siècle* artists on the side of the new architecture. In 1882 we find Oscar Wilde telling an audience that 'all machinery may be beautiful ... the line of strength and the line of beauty being one'. Walter Crane, a few years later, was saying much the same thing.

Thus we have the two movements – often confused, in fact diametrically opposed. One, the strict craft approach of men like Voysey, Webb or Gimson, in the Morris tradition; two, Van der Velde's and Horta's theory of 'invented' ornament – those languid curves redolent of Swinburnian passion.

Both movements, as we see now, were impossible. The Morris doctrine could not ultimately exist in an age geared to the machine and to a metallic architecture. Architectural *Art Nouveau* could not ultimately exist since ornament – as with the tracery, ribs or mullions of Gothic – must have at least some rational basis in function or structure. In any 'total architecture' function, ornament and structure are absolutely integrated; *Art Nouveau* ornament does not conform to this definition; it is something added to the structure. That unresolved conflict between two ultimately impossible movements haunted the last years of the century.

Not even a genius could truly resolve that conflict. Which is a pity since the genius was forthcoming. His name was Charles Rennie

107 C.R.Mackintosh: The drawing-room, the Mackintoshes' studio flat, 120 Main Street, Glasgow. *The Mackintoshes' own studio ... Art Nouveau at its height. Mackintosh's wife regretted his concern with architecture at the expense – as she thought – of decoration. This room, therefore, may be as much hers as his.*

Mackintosh (1868–1928) and he emerged in, of all unlikely places, Glasgow. '*Si j'étais Dieu!*' were the words which the French architect, Mallet Stephens, placed over his door. 'And if you were God?' he was asked. 'Then,' he said, 'I should design like Mackintosh.' Mackintosh, the son of a Glasgow policeman, made his way to the local art school where, with the aid of that tycoon of art education, Fra Newberry, he became one of a group who were to be famous ... even if their fame was destined to be greater in Vienna or Zurich than in Scotland. Into that *Art Nouveau* world of swooning and anarchic forms, and memories of Rossetti maidens, more than one continental architect plunged disastrously – disastrously, because architecture, being structural, must never be anarchic. Mackintosh plunged too, but kept his head.

How nearly Mackintosh came to reconciling the two movements, or at least how far he recognized the merits of both, is shown in his own work. In the *interior* of the houses he built around Glasgow he saw a legitimate field for non-structural decoration, and there, in the stencilled patterns, appliqué textiles, beaten copper and so on, he and his wife were quite uninhibited. The *exterior* of those houses was another matter. Mackintosh here showed a strict regard for the principles of the Arts and Crafts movement, an almost puritanical structural integrity. One, at least, of those houses, Windyhill, Kilmacolm (1899) is almost indistinguishable from the work of Voysey, while yet another, Hill House, Helensburgh, is even more austere.

In the late nineties, to woo the Glasgow clerks from their whisky, a Miss Cranston opened a series of famous tea-rooms, designed to attract [108]. Here again, Mackintosh saw scope for full-blooded *Art Nouveau* decoration. Tall, willowy Pre-Raphaelite maidens, complete with lilies, are stencilled on the walls of one restaurant; a sparkling cluster of test-tubes form the light fitting of another, chairs and tableware and panelling are all typical of *Art Nouveau* at its highest development. One or two tea-rooms remain almost as museum pieces.

Mackintosh, contrary to what is often supposed, did little work abroad, but his European reputation was immense. In 1900 he and his wife designed an apartment in the Vienna Secessionist Exhibition – brilliant in colour, complete with gesso panels and all the apparatus of *Art Nouveau* ornament. True, by that time Mackintosh's reputation had been enhanced by his main work, the Glasgow Art School, but

even so, looking now at the old photographs of this apartment and remembering its date, one can almost understand the enthusiasm it produced. When the Mackintoshes arrived in Vienna the students drew them through the city in a flower-decked carriage.

In 1896 Mackintosh won the competition for Glasgow's new Art School. Sir John Summerson has said that all Mackintosh did was to attenuate otherwise ordinary building forms to resemble the *Art Nouveau* lily on its slender stalk. This is untenable. Mackintosh may have attenuated parts of his building to achieve 'exquisiteness' as many classicists before him had done to achieve 'elegance'. But he was never of the 'Yellow Book' temperament, he was a sound Scottish builder. If the Art School's famous library, with its glitter, colour and delicious fuss, is a decorator's *tour de force* [109], the building itself is a most masculine essay in square-cut stone, iron and plate glass – all in a hard-headed Scottish tradition [110]. An occasional twist in the ironwork may 'date' but otherwise the structural starkness is almost dour, the magnificently lit studios altogether functional. The exterior qualities come from a dramatic contrast of window and plain wall – not from the ornament, which is actually negligible. Apart from the decoration and the furniture upon which so much of Mackintosh's fame now rests, the Art School was really his only important architectural work. The Committee had asked for a 'plain' building. They landed themselves with a *succès de scandale*. Oddly enough they also got what they had asked for. That rather uncompromising pile of stone and iron has roots going deep into the nineteenth century; it is also a bridge between the years before the First World War and the years after it. It was labelled *Art Nouveau* but it contains far more of Walter Gropius than it does of Aubrey Beardsley. It was also the last great monument of the Victorian Age.

204

109 C.R. Mackintosh: The Art School, Glasgow, library

110 C.R. Mackintosh: The Art School, Glasgow, entrance

9

The House

If the town-halls, the churches, the railway stations and the cities themselves tell the story of a great nation in a state both of fervent achievement and of flux – the story of a new-born romanticism at war with a new technology ... then the story of the house is the story of individual men, not in isolation from the main theme of life, but expressing their private reactions to that theme in terms of architecture.

That those reactions might be personal and even eccentric, as indeed they often were; that they might be a gesture of defiance, a protest against all accepted canons of taste, reveals the age no less certainly than does some dreary architectural expression of the norm. Wyatt's 'Abbey' for Beckford at the beginning of the century, like Godwin's White House for Whistler towards the end, tell us more about their very different epochs than do all the houses of conformity.

The house itself, like the books on the shelves and the pictures on the walls, is an outward and visible statement about its owner – but that owner, in some sense or other, is also a child of his time. The house, therefore, although 'private' is, no less than other buildings, a social phenomenon ... perhaps more than any.

For centuries the position of the private patron and his architect, the whole method of house building – whatever minor fashions of style might ripple the smooth waters of a classical culture – had remained undisturbed. (This statement is subject, of course, to the all-important proviso that it applies only at those very high social levels where an architect was employed at all. The vast majority of Englishmen, buried as they were in the villages and market towns, had certainly never seen and perhaps hardly heard of such a rarified creature as 'an architect' – at least until Queen Victoria was upon the throne.) The architect, like other artists, had for too long been an uncritically accepted figure of his time; he was on the band-wagon, as universally accepted, if also as nearly anonymous, as the aircraft designer today. He was neither controversial nor even 'interesting'. In any case to be too interested in anything or anyone was, most emphatically, not an eighteenth-century attitude.

Only rarely did the architect of those earlier centuries rise above anonymity; very rarely was he acclaimed. And even then, as when Pembroke instructed Inigo Jones at Wilton or when Lord Carlisle directed Vanbrugh at Castle Howard – they were little more than what we might call 'technical advisers' – even if a part of their expertise, as would be assumed, might lie in the sphere of current fashion – the Italianate, the Palladian or what you will. They were not less eclectic than those Victorians who have so often been accused of eclecticism. It was merely that the wheel of fashion turned a little slower.

Eighteenth-century architects, therefore, although not without honour, bore the status of technicians, as against the status of 'gentlemen' – which belonged to those they served. The University of Oxford – virtually an eighteenth-century institution – to this day, save for one lectureship of nineteenth-century foundation, teaches no art; it prefers, still, to train not artists but gentlemen who will be the patrons of artists.

That the façade of the eighteenth-century mansion should be compiled from classical elements was, at least for educated or 'polite' people, as normal as that a painter or even a poet should look to antique models. Style, in that sense, was a thing that one could, in the Augustan Age, discuss with complete detachment, certainly without either the emotion or the passion so necessary to great art. It was only in the fully-fledged Victorian Age – when the Romantic Movement and the Industrial Revolution between them had transformed the world – that style became something over which one had to agonize, an issue at least as theological and moral as it was aesthetic.

This pseudo-menial status of the architect was something which Nash, through his dubious friendship with the Regent, had tried to change. He had been unsuccessful. After all, his predecessors – if few in number – had also hobnobbed with princes. If this situation was to change – and it was not necessarily desirable that it should – it would, in the end, change through a new attitude to architecture, not to architects. It was a cultural issue, not a social one ... and it is cultural changes which, though more momentous, work more slowly in the earth. For Nash to dine now and then at the Brighton Pavilion was not in itself going to make the ordinary Englishman trouble himself overmuch about the 'style' of his house – or even to employ an architect at all. *That*, oddly enough, involved a revolution of the mind towards both God and Man.

And that could not happen overnight. Far on into the nineteenth century, when an architect visited his private patron he would – like any curate, bailiff or dentist – dine in the housekeeper's room. An angry and embittered Pugin – although his dream master-mason might have been even more humiliated – did ultimately move on terms of equality with Lord Shrewsbury and thus, not unhappily, built the fantastic towers of Alton, as well as a dozen gilded chancels. It was left, however, to Charles Barry to stir himself in favour of the gentleman architect; and it was Gilbert Scott – with all the drawings for the restoration of Salisbury in the *tonneau* of his coach – who bowled up to the Bishop's Palace with postilions and outrider.

Now all this, oddly enough, had an architectural significance. If all the romanticism and deliberately affected historical stylism really symbolized a collapse in taste, they also symbolized, what was more important, an intensification of the imagination. They meant that the architect was often, paradoxically, a more Bohemian, more individualistic person than hitherto. He could no longer be taken for granted as a species of superior country builder just able to draw a Palladian façade – which was all that most eighteenth-century architects ever were. Whether among stern and unbending Tories, among Gothically inclined priests and eccentrics or among industrial *nouveaux riches* – painters, poets, novelists, architects were now at least controversial figures. They were discussed. They might be laughed at – *Punch* still laughs at them – and the Royal Academy might dislike them – it still does – but their names were known and they were sometimes held in regard ... if not often in very high regard. Sometimes they were even – as Coleridge would have claimed – a kind of curious link with God.

The Victorian patron – with all the styles open to him wherewith to make a social splash, to express his high thinking or his fine feeling – often chose the architect of his own house with care. The choice – had the householder read Ruskin – was clearly a moral one. And, even at a slightly less rarified level than that, to buy Pre-Raphaelite paintings, to hear Pusey's sermons, to read Browning, to employ a Charles Barry or a Philip Webb, according to the 'set' or circle in which you moved – those innumerable converging and yet exclusive circles of Victorian society – was something that was most emphatically, as we would say, 'done'.

This highly individualistic and subjective kind of patronage we have already discovered (Chapter 4) in our examination of the first phase of the Gothic Revival. And the first of those patrons – himself more romantic and more eccentric than any architect he could find – was certainly the most eccentric. In the building of that sham and gimcrack pile of Gothic scenery, below the last slopes of Salisbury plain, William Beckford – within the limits of his day and with an inadequate architect – did nothing of importance except make a gesture. Misanthropic, homosexual, twisted and temperamental Beckford might be, but Fonthill – Strawberry Hill having been little more than a series of archaeological interiors – was a tremendous gesture against the world, a thumbing of the nose at the whole System, at Society no less than at Society's art. Preceding the romantic poets – whether in the Lake District or in Weimar – by more than a generation, it was the first shot in a battle that Beckford could never live to understand. It might all be a gesture of thwarted eccentricity rather than of a great imagination ... but primarily it *was* a gesture and as such was of significance. Its plan, with the central octagonal lobby was to influence the Palace at Westminster; the picturesque grouping of its masses was a further step in the progress of the Gothic Revival. Primarily, however, Fonthill was not an essay in design by an architect; it was a statement by a patron. It was also a very personal statement, and as such was a nineteenth- not an eighteenth-century thing. Houses, henceforth, were not to be judged by such refinements of design as their façades might display – they were, rather, to be statements, often very revealing statements, about the people who built them and lived in them.

James Wyatt, an idle man with some power of design and a knowledge of Gothic, could never fully interpret Beckford's wild dream. Only when architect and patron were matched could the nineteenth-century house be truly launched. It was not until Scarisbrick in 1837 – when Pugin's richly dight gables and towers at last stood in the Lancashire marches – that the rich and eccentric patron was served by a fanatical genius. Neither Scarisbrick nor Pugin cared of course, as an eighteenth-century scholar would have cared, for anything so cool as design – a merely seemly arrangement of established forms. Again, we have a gesture, a proclamation, about history, life, religion. It is this proclamation that overwhelms every other consideration.

It was, therefore, that most symbolic figure of the new society – the romantic eccentric – who initiated the new style. Gothic might have remained a mere *specialité d'église* – beloved only of the Camden Society, of Puseyites and Old Catholics, an accompaniment for incense and illicit confession – if these slightly insane eccentrics, such as Beckford and Shrewsbury, had not built themselves vast residential abbeys. Between the *Castle of Otranto* and the homes of Hampstead stockbrokers there is a clear but curious continuity.

Rapidly, thereafter, Gothic became the style of a hundred less poetic, but not smaller, mansions, until in the end even the suburban stucco terraces of West Kensington or St John's Wood could forget their putative father – Nash of the Terraces – in order to acquire steep gables and to divide the plate glass with mullions.

The rustic cottage, the *cottage ornée*, the estate village and the Gothic lodge have been overemphasized. Once granted the Gothic and castellated mansion, then these things were no more than garden and park ornaments, naturally partaking of the style of the big house. As temples, pyramids and a baroque mausoleum had, long ago, adorned the park at Castle Howard, as had a Roman bridge at Blenheim, a Palladian one at Wilton; so the 'picturesque' was a similarly natural extension of Gothic to smaller or more bucolic things.

The era of the Napoleonic Wars, accompanied by an upsurge of nationalism, had seen a whole series of large and well-ordered mansions, disguised rather ineffectively as feudal castles. The precious heritage of Little Lord Fauntleroy, they were all an expression of that high Tory pride in 'lineage' which, as we have seen, was at least one facet of romanticism – important mainly because it transferred the Gothic passion from the rebel left wing to the Establishment – thus opening the way to more official uses of the style and to its general acceptance for domestic architecture.

At Ashridge (1808–17) in Hertfordshire – with its battlemented and machicolated perimeter wall, its crowning flêches over the great hall, with the minstrels' gallery and suspended cast-iron stair, and lovely 'perpendicular' chapel – Wyatt had built perhaps the greatest, certainly the loveliest, of these castles.

The towers of Eastnor – a castle that the ghost of Edward III would almost take for granted – still lie poetically and deliberately poised beneath the Malvern Hills; while in Leicestershire only the excessive fenestration of the picturesque pile that stands on Belvoir's terraces betrays the fact that this is for house parties rather than for archers.

All this, of course, was no more Victorian in actual date than was Nash's curiously Norman essay in the desmesne at Killymoon (1803), his own comfortable but well-castellated home in East Cowes (c. 1798), or even Robert Adam's Culzean of the previous century ... these houses were the initiators, the curtain-raisers to the full drama of romantic home-building which died only with Lutyens, Lloyd Wright, and the Tudor suburbs of the inter-war years. Such houses became outmoded ultimately, less because of changes in fashion, taste or style, less because of their inherent unreality and absurdity, than because the sort of people for whom they were built were fortunately eliminated from society. Against the Victorian background of emerging industrialists, those landed and feudal gentry may seem sometimes to be no more than an eighteenth-century hangover; in fact, as builders of great houses – though decreasingly as wielders of power – they were a social reality at least until 1914.

Just as Gothic Revival church-building went through a whole series of phases, each with its own emphasis – style, archaeology, function, structure, craftsmanship – so also with the house.

The first step was the rather shattering realization that, in the Victorian sense of the word, there had never been such a thing as a Gothic house. (Equally, although designed in vast quantities throughout the nineteenth century [113], there had never been such a thing as Gothic

111 M. D. Wyatt: Alford House. *A fashionable Kensington house designed by the last of the Wyatt dynasty, and in his old age at that. It is not unskilful, but it shows that Wyatt was quite untouched by a current change in the architectural outlook.*

112 Thomas Cubitt: Osborne House. *Thomas Cubitt, unlike his brothers, was a builder rather than an architect. He drew the plans for this royal retreat, but as the real architect was alleged to have been Prince Albert, Cubitt's status and the design itself are explained.*

furniture.) The castle – the only piece of medieval domesticity on a conveniently feudal scale – had, after all, been only a fort. The merchant's house of the later medieval towns – in spite of such real gems as the Greville House at Chipping Campden or the inn at Glastonbury – seemed to offer no kind of useful precedent for the suburban home. The manor house, as a model for imitation, might seem to us rather nearer the mark. This was not so. The early Victorians were not interested in either simplicity or craftsmanship. Whereas the manor had been an essay in the vernacular – distinguishable from the yeoman's farm only by the provision of a few more rooms and an occasional heraldic beast – to Pugin and his successors Gothic meant, *per se*, carving and enrichment. To transfer to desirable residences all that ecclesiastical enrichment – which of course could never have existed save to the glory of the Undivided Trinity – was as absurd as it was zealous. It is, however, the explanation as to why a hundred Victorian houses are as they are.

As we have seen, at Fonthill, Scarisbrick, Alton and the feudal castles, this zealous absurdity was indulged without inhibition. Then came the doubts and the evasions. If medievalism could be thought of – and it often was – as ending not with the Reformation but with the 'Great Rebellion' then all manner of courses were open. We have noted, for instance, that 'Elizabethan' was offered to the competitors as an alternative to 'Gothic' in designing the Palace of Westminster. If 'Elizabethan' was ideologically anathema to Catholics or High Anglicans, it was at least - in an era of high self-confidence – 'national' enough to be part of the great romantic myth. And no one could deny that the Elizabethans had built houses and mansions.

The prolific era of eclecticism and style-mixing now began. The vagaries of style between one man's work and another; the vagaries of style between one man's work this year and his work next year, did nothing whatever to diminish the passionate conviction that this manner of building rather than that was correct – morally, historically and functionally correct. A sketching tour was a sufficient basis for a new dispensation ... for a complete change in the pattern of the London streets.

When Pugin's Scarisbrick, for a Catholic squire, was still rising,

113 Upholsterer's catalogue: Grand piano in 'Gothic Style'

Anthony Salvin was building at Harlaxton in Lincolnshire a vast assemblage of courts and halls – a monstrous Hatfield – all in an accomplished version of the heretic style of Queen Elizabeth.

In Scotland, which shared only with Weimar the honour of being the fount of romanticism, castle-building went on a little longer than in the South. All the impact of Waverley, Jacobitism and Border romance existed not – like the Gothic novel in England – as a series of literary associations, but as a genuine force that had never quite died. Side by side with the neo-Grec and the Edinburgh philosophers, the picturesque and the medieval flourished. They are there, literally side by side, in Prince's Street. The fantasy towers of many castles look down upon the Border or upon the Valley of the Tweed; and in the sixties, long after the English had dropped such excesses, the power of Walter Scott, added to the power of a German upbringing, compelled Prince Albert to purchase and to enlarge Balmoral [114]. The consequent Baronial style, with its pepperpot turrets, its stepped gables, and overtones of peel towers and the old French alliance, is to be found not only in seaside boarding-houses, but also, unfortunately, in the work of Sir Edward Lorrimer through the first quarter of the present century.

If we accept the usual theory – which can be done only with major

114 William Smith: Balmoral

qualifications – that the Victorian Age saw a collapse in taste; that collapse is best shown in the work of Charles Barry (1795–1860). From that thesis we can exclude Barry's great life work, the Palace of Westminster, remembering always what that building owed to Pugin ... so far as taste is concerned, almost all. In judging Barry's role in the story of the English house, we must also recall – what is seldom mentioned – that two of the finest Gothic residences of the age – the Speaker's and the Lord Chancellor's houses – are buried in the Westminster conglomeration.

Westminster apart, Barry's career shows a distressing decline in taste, an increasing desire to provide 'effects', an increasing snobbery in plan, an increasing reliance upon ornament which, in itself, became increasingly coarse-grained. A certain magnificence in the basic concept was preserved to the end.

In his two Pall Mall clubs – the Travellers' (1830) and the Reform (1837) – Barry made a genuine and indeed successful effort to marry Greek austerity with the splendour of the Roman Renaissance. Apart from the inherent improbability of putting a glass roof over an Italian *cortile*, and the inadequacy of Roman fenestration in the pale London sunlight, these two buildings – simple, astylar, grand – are landmarks in domestic architecture.

Thereafter, something – perhaps Barry's own facile handling of detail, perhaps an excessive awareness of his own professional status or of the rank of his clients, perhaps an excess of commissions – would seem to have gone to his head. Wolfe, his closest friend, said of Barry that not only was his taste for ornament 'remarkable', but that to the end of his career 'he seemed to think that enrichment could never be overdone'. He thought that ornament, like the hieroglyphics and reliefs on an Egyptian temple, should be everywhere. If, as has been suggested, Barry got his idea of 'all-over' ornament from the patina of Perpendicular panelling that covers the wall surfaces at Westminster, it only shows that Pugin understood the true nature of Gothic much better than Barry.

This obsession with ornament is found not only on Barry's public buildings, as in Whitehall, but in the great houses – town and country – which, through the forties and fifties, he was building for the nobility.

Ornamentation was accompanied by an anarchic idea of style, a truly extraordinary eclecticism. Not only did Barry move from style to style in different buildings – as notably but excusably between Westminster and Pall Mall – but from style to style in the same building!

Within a year of completing the Reform Club – with all its external austerity – Barry was reconstructing Highclere in Hampshire for the Earl of Caernarvon. Highclere could hardly be called 'austere'. Highclere, like the Palace of Westminster, has a notable and dramatic skyline – the towers and the turrets continuing rather splendidly the 'Elizabethan' massing of a great house, as Salvin had used it at Harlaxton. Otherwise, however, Highclere is usually described as 'Jacobean'. That is to be kind.

Ten years after the Reform Club, Barry was building Bridgewater House for the Earl of Ellesmere. This town mansion, looking on to the Green Park, was only one of that great series – Devonshire House, Dorchester House, Grosvenor House, Bridgewater House, Stafford House – erected over a period of a hundred years, for the display, the conspicuous waste and the self-adulation of a ruling-class. To this series Barry who – like Lutyens a generation later – loved the rich contributed more than his share.

115 W.H.Crossland: Royal Holloway College. *This millionaire's mansion – now a college – was one of the real* tours-de-force *of High Victorianism. The architect took the lushest of all historical styles – that of the chateaux of the Loire Valley – and interpreted it in English brick, without any inhibitions whatever. The skyline is almost as impressive as that of Chambord.*

Bridgewater House, like the Reform Club, had a roofed *cortile*. There the resemblance ended. The exterior, with its large corner chimney stacks and clumsy attic storey, was coarse. Internally it gave an opportunity for what Barry's son described as 'a desire for great richness of effect' – mainly a most costly display of splendid arabesques by Crace.

To Stafford House (now Lancaster House) Barry added a grand staircase for the Duke of Sutherland. The inevitable comparison with the earlier interiors by Benjamin Wyatt, is unfavourable to Barry. Nevertheless, this stair, significantly beloved by Disraeli, is still one of the finest things of its kind to survive in London. It even impresses the visiting statesmen and diplomats for whose reception it is now a setting. It drew from Queen Victoria her remark to the Duchess that 'I come from my home [117] to your palace'.

For the same ducal patron, in 1845, Barry had drastically re-modelled Dunrobin Castle on the Sutherland coast. On a wild and rocky northern shore the romantic skyline of the 'Baronial' style comes into its own – a relief after the artificialities and boring Italian gardens of Harewood, Cliveden, Trentham [118] or Shrublands. For all that, these great houses by Barry cannot be ignored in the story of Victorian architecture. In a prolific age they are very typical of a little of what is good and of much that is bad.

Before Barry's career had ended a subtle change was already in the air. If Barry and Waterhouse – as for instance in the latter's egregious Eaton Hall of 1867–80 [119, 120] – had symbolized High Victorianism in domestic architecture, what was now to matter far more was a whole series of architects of a different kind – Norman Shaw (1831–1912), Philip Webb (1831–1915), Eden Nesfield (1835–88), W. R. Lethaby (1857–1931), C. F. A. Voysey (1857–1941), Baillie Scott (1865–1945), Edwin Lutyens (1869–1944) ... and so on into the twentieth century and our own day.

These architects, being children of their time, could hardly avoid some sort of deference to some sort of historical style; and, indeed, Norman Shaw, the outstanding figure, was the most eclectic of all the architects that ever were. Nevertheless, these men were concerned not primarily with the imitation or even interpretation of a style – whether Gothic or Italian – but rather with certain basic questions

117 John Nash, Edward Blore *et al.*: Buckingham Palace, The Bow Library. *Palace interiors, as one would expect, try to sit on the fence – to be both fashionable and conservative. It is not possible. Personal rooms – boudoirs, studies, etc. – may sometimes have a sentimental interest. Otherwise, as here, the effect is one of monumental dullness and pomposity.*

118 Charles Barry: Trentham Hall. *For the Duke of Sutherland Barry built Stafford House in London, Dunrobin Castle in Scotland, and Trentham Hall (now demolished) in Staffordshire. It was a huge pseudo-Italian affair, with vast and ornate formal gardens. This kind of garden must be thought of as filling the gap between the 'picturesque' era of Payne Knight and Paxton, and the Jekyll era of the herbaceous border and the enlightened amateur.*

119 Alfred Waterhouse: Eaton Hall. *The expression of tremendous wealth and self-assurance inherent in High Victorianism is justifiable in, say, the public buildings of Manchester; in a private house it is merely vulgar. Even Waterhouse cannot prevent this.*

120 Alfred Waterhouse: Eaton Hall. *The desire to express noble blood and lineage, both in the Gothic style of the stair and in the display of armour, is – like the house itself – either very vulgar or perhaps, at this distance of time, comic.*

about the nature of architecture – with function, materials, craftsmanship, plan and beauty. The change was not, perhaps, after all so very subtle; it was fundamental.

It is now fashionable to assert that the Red House (Chapter 7) which Philip Webb built for William Morris as early as 1859, was not such a significant landmark as has been supposed. True, it was not recognized as such in 1859. (That is the usual fate of any piece of progressive architecture.) But if we take everything into account – the social as well as the architectural implications of the Red House, its significance *was* profound. Until then the architecture of the great Victorian houses had consisted mainly of the imposition of new stylistic variations upon basically eighteenth-century themes. With the Red House, with Philip Webb, with the emergence of the young Norman Shaw and with Morrisian ideals of craftsmanship hovering, as it were, in the wings, the change is obvious. Far off we can sniff the twentieth century upon the wind.

For one thing the change was social. It was a change of patronage. If men like Barry had troubled themselves to establish the social status of the architect that was no more than recognition by them that the eighteenth-century class structure was trying to perpetuate itself into a century where, clearly, it was destined to die. Barry and his like loved a lord, and built for lords. But the cool, rational eighteenth-century mind – concerned with 'taste' but indifferent to what others thought – was no longer enough. Barry, through architecture, had to make, for his patrons, the last great gesture. These London palaces of the Victorian hostesses, these country mansions of the big house parties, were *meant* to express social grandeur. And this last self-assertion of a dying aristocracy was necessarily vulgar. The aristocratic principle could no longer be taken for granted; it had to draw attention to itself.

Now, by the sixties, this particular force was almost played out. From 1865 Burges, at Cardiff Castle, was supplying the Marquis of Bute with a set of highly Gothicized, highly coloured and altogether sumptuous interiors. In the years that followed, both Norman Shaw and – towards the end of the century – Lutyens, were to cater now and again, for some astounding ostentation – but that ostentation became less and less the insignia of lineage or rank, and perhaps less vulgar. The new kind of client *might* be ducal; he was more likely to be industrial. Norman Shaw still built occasionally for the aristocratic remnant ... for a Portman he built the vast pile of Bryanston on the hill above Blandford; but at Cragside in Northumberland [121], as early as 1870, he built a fantasia of gables and chimneys for Armstrong, the Newcastle steelmaster ... while Lutyens, in his earlier years, built fairly consistently for Sugar, Soap, Grocery and Textiles. These new patrons were not the philistine and illiterate bosses of the earlier railway boom; in denying their birth they asserted their education and, just a few of them – in London as in Chicago – were men of taste and patrons of the arts.

We can indeed sniff the twentieth century upon the wind! And yet it still remains absurd to call Norman Shaw 'a pioneer of the modern movement' – as has been done. True, he abandoned, for the eternal good of architecture, both the archaeological restraints and the rich grossness of High Victorianism, substituting for it an architecture more charming, more sensitive, more functional, more original ... although *not* more modern. Shaw was an historicist, and an almost

121 R. Norman Shaw: Cragside

bewildering eclectic of the first order. So far from being even faintly 'modern' there is – bar full Gothic – hardly a style in the history books that he was not capable of adapting brilliantly to his own purpose.

He was born in 1831, and by 1863 was already in partnership with Eden Nesfield. Each man worked on his own, and since Nesfield was averse to publicity it is difficult to sort out their work – not that it is important. It is certain that Nesfield's larger houses, such as Cloverley Hall, Shropshire (1862) and Kinmell Park in Wales, had a profound influence upon Shaw … and thus indirectly upon the whole English domestic scene. Nesfield's Cloverley, for instance, was a quite fantastic essay in huge mullioned Tudor windows – virtually window-walls – gables and chimney stacks. Although vaguely medieval it is a complete break with the use, in domestic architecture, of that full ecclesiastic Gothic – the only way in which Pugin's generation could show their deference to the Middle Ages. Although so much larger and grander than the Red House it is a tribute to the vernacular of the English manor. As such it is a break with the immediate past, a forerunner of both Shaw and Lutyens. It is also a pointer to the fact that the new kind of patron would have liked an old yeoman's house if only it were possible to fit inside it all the kitchens, nurseries, gun-rooms and stables that were the paraphernalia of modern life a century ago.

It was this marriage between a simple vernacular and the elaborate ritual of late Victorian family life that was the basis of Shaw's best work. In this sense he was a bridge between the gross grandeur of Barry's generation and the 'simple-life' of Voysey and the Garden Cities. Sociologically and philosophically like the nineteenth century itself, the whole thing was an absurdity. It was, however, a suitable and fascinating vehicle for a brilliant display of Shavian architectural fireworks.

How absurd, how brilliant, is shown by asking any man his view of the 'typical' Norman Shaw style. There is, of course, no such thing. Everyone will give his own answer.

First: there is a house such as Leys Wood, near Groombridge (1868) in the 'Sussex style' – all tile-hanging, barge boards, sham half-timbering and long ranges of casements. Its shams and its pretentiousness must have sickened Morris or Webb. In its medieval richness

122 R. Norman Shaw: Dawpool. *One of Norman Shaw's many attempts to adapt the whole paraphernalia of the English vernacular – gables, chimneys, mullions, buttresses and all – to a building intended primarily for the use of large and fashionable house parties. Shaw almost pulled it off; in lesser hands it was disastrous. (This house has been demolished.)*

123 R. Norman Shaw: 185 Queen's Gate. *A Tudor Town house is something of a contradiction in terms ... if this is Tudor. It is the skilful use of areas of plain brick-work against rich fenestration that gives the house its two main characteristics – good scale and quality. (Destroyed by bombs.)*

it is still close to Nesfield's Cloverley, but also – though ducal in scale – the ancestor of all the suburban 'Stockbroker's Tudor' that was yet to come. Shaw was to design plenty more Leys Woods, returning to this dubious first love again and again.

Four years later, however, he is back to Nesfield's bastard 'Queen Anne', plus a mixture of 'Ipswich oriels', cut-brick and Dutch gables. This, to most people, is the nearest thing to a 'typical' Norman Shaw style. It is immensely cosy and nostalgic. It unfortunately demands craftsmen and hand-made materials which, at that date, were seldom available. In this manner Shaw built his own home, in 1875, at Ellerdale Road, Hampstead, also New Zealand Chambers in Leadenhall Street in 1872 [124], and in the next year Lowther Lodge, Kensington Gore – now the earlier wing of the Geographical Society's house.

Most lovely and most significant was Swan House, Chelsea, in 1876 [125]. The same elements were here combined, but in a much more masterly way. The ground and first floor are almost wholly glazed and form a rich lower band – a sort of podium upon which stands the high

124 R. Norman Shaw:
New Zealand Chambers

125 R. Norman Shaw: Swan House

second-floor *piano nobile*, its height emphasized by its fenestration – a series of tall oriels set in plain brick. This vertical storey is, again, topped by a continuous band of lesser windows. Here, therefore, style is quite secondary; it is the broad composition that matters – the solids against the voids, the verticals against the horizontals. That is something elementary, but it is also something which modern architects – lacking the crutch of historical precedent – have had to come back to. In five minutes a deft draftsman could redesign Swan House as a modern building ... which is not to say that Shaw had any 'modern' predilections. He had not. It was simply that, now and again, the artist within him was stronger than the historian.

This occasional mastery of *real*, as opposed to stylistic design, makes all the sadder Shaw's later eclectic orgies. In his later years Shaw was responsible for an Edwardian–Imperial–Baroque. In the era of King Edward, the South African diamond millionaires and the Chicago heiresses, he was never such a foolish architect as Herbert Baker, never so brashly Parisian as Méwes and Davis at the Ritz; never, on the

other hand, was he on the side of the angels. Neither the Arts and Crafts, nor *Art Nouveau*, nor the Yellow Book ever knew him. He was fashionable and successful. So there came that megalomaniac moment in his career – it came to Lutyens at Heathcote, Ilkley in 1906 – when he suddenly felt he must go 'baroque'. It was in 1891 that he designed Chesters in Northumberland ... with its concave façades, huge detached columns and rustications. This was Reginald Bloomfield's favourite Shaw house; in truth it stands only for a not very mighty mind o'erthrown. The Piccadilly Hotel (1905) [126] – although, strictly, irrelevant to our period – is still an astonishing pyrotechnical display of versatility in detail ... and yet, as Nikolaus Pevsner says, 'it is a display of diminished power'.

It is Shaw's enormous house for the Duke of Portman at Bryanston (1890) [127] – an essay in what has been facetiously called the 'Wrenaissance' style – that symbolizes as well as anything the passing of the architectural initiative from England to the United States. There was still to be that extraordinary one-man epilogue of the Lutyens dream houses; there were still to be the Garden Cities and the whole aftermath of the Arts and Crafts and *Das Englisch Haus*. But it is

127 R. Norman Shaw: Bryanston

Bryanston, with its brash and assertive pattern of crimson brick and white stone, set on one of the noblest sites an architect was ever given, high in the woods above a Dorset vale, that can be held to symbolize the trans-Atlantic shift.

That absurd house, for all its tremendous panache, never even begins to be married to its marvellous site. It stands well enough, in an obvious way, right on top of the hill, but it could just as easily be somewhere else. It is on the hill, not part of it. That very tender marriage between architecture and the earth – as we see it in Spanish castles, in Venice, in Cotswold villages and Umbrian hill towns – is really all that Lloyd Wright ever meant by 'organic architecture'. And when Norman Shaw and Lutyens, all unawares, were trying in vain to escape from the irrelevant shackles of Queen Anne mansions and Sussex manors, Lloyd Wright – even then – thanks to Thoreau and Walt Whitman, was really and truly understanding Art and Man and the Soil. He was building houses in Pennsylvanian forests or in the Arizona desert that were both fundamental and primeval, as well as infinitely sophisticated. The English house was strangling itself with the entrails of its own past glories.

If Norman Shaw had been the central figure of the seventies and eighties – in succession to such High Victorians as Barry – the last decades were dominated by C.F.A.Voysey (1857–1941). While both men, with their admiration for the English vernacular, were in a sense disciples of Philip Webb, they were also very different from each other. With the transition from Shaw to Voysey we find ourselves in a sweeter and simpler world. Or was it after all, one may well ask – the simplicity being so contrived – merely a more sophisticated world?

Like Norman Shaw, Voysey has been claimed as a 'pioneer of the Modern Movement'. Both claims are dubious. While Shaw was the supreme historicist and eclectic, Voysey, it is true, was something of a 'functionalist' both in the designing of forms 'fit for their purpose' and in his rigid insistence upon good materials. But neither of those things are in themselves 'modern', nor was the austerity which derives quite simply from the fact that Voysey's earlier clients were Quakers, and he himself of a puritan cast of mind. Voysey lived long enough to loathe 'modern architecture' – the inaugural exhibition of the MARS Group, in his last years, made him ill. The white stucco, used only to be sure of waterproof walls, and the long horizontal bands of case-ments – Tudor anyway – were the only motifs which can, even remotely, justify the word 'modern'.

The claim that Voysey was an *Art Nouveau* architect is also very slim. Vertical members, it is true, were often attenuated; the exag-gerated cyma moulding often used – both sign manuals of *Art Nouveau*. But in fact and in spirit no one – positively no one – could have been further from the world of the 'Yellow Book' and the Café Royal, and yet be actually alive in London at the same time. No, it was Charles Rennie Mackintosh (Chapter 8) who, in prosperous subur-ban Glasgow, managed to combine a stern Scottish functionalism externally with, internally, a joyous riot of *Art Nouveau* excess. And it was E.W.Godwin (1833–86) builder of Dromore Castle in Ireland and of the White House in Chelsea for Whistler, who must be regarded – however ephemeral his fame – as the true architect of the *fin-de-siècle*. Voysey can, perhaps, be understood best as a disciple of Morris who faced the facts of life as Morris never could. Like Morris, Voysey believed in the revival of the crafts. In the last analysis his furniture, tableware and textiles may prove to be better than his houses. He faced the facts – as Morris did not – about the real nature and integrity of medieval building. If Voysey used square stone mullions it was not because they were more 'functional' – chamfered mullions let in more light – but because he was unwilling to ask a craftsman to carve what the craftsman could not design.

That tradition of craftsmanship inaugurated by Morris, that integrity of structure derived from Lethaby and from Philip Webb, that whimsical charm of Baillie Scott, that new kind of professional-ism founded so emphatically by Barry and upheld by Norman Shaw ... could all these diverse threads be drawn together into any kind of architectural unity? At least the attempt was made. Edwin Lutyens (1869–1944), like so many famous architects, had little formal train-ing. Early in life, through the Lytton family, he married into a charmed circle of wealth and taste. He then created an epilogue to five centuries of country-house building. Those famous dream houses – built around the turn of the century – Munstead Wood [128], Deanery Garden, Papillon Hall and all the rest – with Gertrude Jekyll's even more dreamlike gardens, will remain as a most curious monument,

128 Edwin Lutyens: Munstead Wood

not to a culture – for they are clean outside their time – but to one man. Like a dream they are unreal, and like a dream they have left not a wrack behind. They were Bernard Shaw's Heartbreak House. They were a gesture from a world where there were still impeccable maids in the Servants' Hall, glossy hunters in the loose boxes, and Peter Pan in the nursery wing. It was all lily ponds, lavender walks and pot-pourri in a Surrey garden. It was also an architecture where the high-pitched roofs, textured stone and tiny casements served mainly to conceal, ever so charmingly, the whole apparatus of conspicuous waste. It all died, as it should have died, in August 1914. Lutyens himself outlived it: with the Cenotaph, the grand manner of New Delhi and the pretentious nonsense of Liverpool's Roman Catholic cathedral, he declined virtually into being no more than a species of Architect Laureate. He was greater than his contemporaries of the same school, but like them he was a dead-end kid.

Twenty years before Lutyens's death Le Corbusier and Lloyd Wright and Gropius and the founding fathers of the Garden Cities

129 81 Banbury Road, Oxford. *Typical North Oxford or, for that matter, typical of any prosperous suburb. These sort of houses – run with, say, three servants, and faintly Ruskinian in tone, were very well suited to married dons.*

were already doing their best work ... and he was probably unaware of their existence. Before the end of the Queen's reign he had made it clear that he was a creative genius ... of sorts. Then he slowly suffocated himself with old traditions, stifled himself with a refusal to face the realities of the twentieth century. He belonged, in fact, neither to the last century nor to this.

In a lecture given at the Geffrye Museum in 1948, the late Mr Goodhart-Rendel said, 'Let us ... leave architecture alone for a moment or two and examine mid-Victorian houses as settings for domestic life.' Now this is a most curious remark. Is not the function of a house to be a setting for domestic life and is not that, therefore and above all things, part of its architecture; or are we to believe that the smaller house is not architecture at all? Or what?

An era's total building output is the whole of its architecture – and by that it must be judged. Without the vernacular of village and cottage we certainly cannot assess the Tudor Age; without the smaller terraces of Georgian country towns we cannot judge the eighteenth century. The Victorian Age paid for its gross prosperity with an excessive population. It was a bitter price, but the result was not only the slum – it was also the suburb, the bye-law streets, the tenements, the 'desirable' villas and the housing estates ... 'development' and all that, today, we still mean by urban sprawl [129]. That sprawl, from top to bottom of the class structure, is part of a single process that has been going on for a hundred and fifty years. The railway, the season ticket and then the internal combustion engine merely hastened it. Even today it is doubtful – such has been the power and ubiquity of 'development' and speculation – whether more than three or four per cent of the houses of England have ever been designed by anyone.

By the date of the Great Exhibition it was realized – if only on the score of pestilence – that the situation was grave. Across the road from the Crystal Palace, therefore, was built a small model block of four tenements – two up and two down – since removed to Kennington. Every room had a window, there was a sink and an external and consequently 'airy' staircase. All this – even if the emphasis was, understandably, upon ventilation rather than amenity – was a tremendous advance. And, unlike the later Garden Cities, it really was built for such of the 'deserving poor' as could be found among the labouring masses. In Letchworth and Bournville [130] and Welwyn there were never any poor ... that had to await the founding of the London County Council in 1889, which, with its own small architect's department, built the first municipal and genuine working-class flats.

From then on we may say that 'housing' – as distinct from houses – existed. There had always been the estate villages, such as Badminton, Harewood or Nash's famous cottages around the green at Blaize – but all these were either mere hovels outside the park gates, or else mere essays in the picturesque, miniature reflections of the architecture of the great houses. An advance was made in 1800, when Paxton designed Edensor, near Chatsworth, for the Duke of Devonshire. Edensor, like all the other estate villages, was designedly picturesque, but the houses themselves were alleged to be 'commodious and comfortable'. Each had water from its own tap and there was sanitation

130 Sycamore Road, Bournville Estate

of an unspecified kind. There was a drying-ground and a playground. About the same time that odd eccentric, the Baroness Burdett-Coutts, was building workers' model dwellings in Bethnal Green, in the shadow of Darbishire's flamboyantly Gothic market. They are still there, still lived in, not quite so 'model' as they were once.

The typical tenement block of philanthropy, however, was produced by the Peabody Trust [131]. Several of these gaunt blocks still remain tucked away behind fashionable West End streets. They perpetuated the open stair and the open access gallery, as well as the railed-in playground. If, to our eyes, they now seen grim and dreary, we must remember that once – a century ago – they were signals from the era of the foetid slum, signals flashed across time to an era in which the State has accepted responsibility for housing every man decently, flashed across time to the era of the Garden City and the New Town.

131 Flats for Peabody Trust, Holborn

10

Modernity is Born

When the clock struck midnight on 31 December 1901, nothing had really happened. When Queen Victoria died at Osborne the next year, nothing had really happened. And yet, even then – with the twentieth century mercifully hidden in the darkness of futurity – it was felt that an epoch had ended.

That that epoch should end at that particular moment was, of course, purely chance. It was clear, however, that the differences between the nineteenth and the twentieth centuries were likely to be fundamental, that it was a change not only from century to century, but from one epoch to another. And the nature of an epoch is that it reverses all the values men have previously held.

Epochal changes are not merely those of, say, technique or taste; they are changes in values. Ancient Rome, with its power, bestiality and efficiency, reversed all the values of the Greek City State; the Middle Ages, with their high systematization of the Sermon on the Mount, reversed all the values of the old Empire; while the Renaissance, when it came, was a mighty secularization of all Europe.

That eternal swing of the pendulum has always been getting quicker, its stroke shorter. Since the end of the Middle Ages – an epoch of some five hundred years – the stroke of the pendulum has approximated to the length of the century. There have been tremendous over-laps and time lags, but for all that the seventeenth and eighteenth and nineteenth centuries were each an epoch. Each offers us a kind of framed vignette of history, each clearly differentiated from the other. Each summons up a picture. Now, today, the pendulum swings even quicker; each generation, almost, reverses the values of its predecessor.

It was clear from the beginning that we, in this century, were destined to reverse and leave behind us all the values of the Victorian

Age – with its transcendental ideal of Progress, and its cultural dominant of Romantic Literature.

Knowing as we do all about institutions of strength sowing the seeds of their own death, we realize – although the Victorians did not – that any belief in an automatic and unlimited Progress – involving supply and demand, Smiles's self-help and *laissez-faire* – could only end in the negation of that Progress. Apart, therefore, from sowing the seeds of death at the peak of achievement – the sowers being Marx, Darwin, Carlyle and Morris – the whole age, like the Roman Empire or the Middle Ages – was self-destructive at its strongest point.

Its full-scale capitalism was so predatory that it ended in Socialism; its domestic respectability so obsessive as to end in all-round sexual emancipation; its philanthropy so intense as to create the Welfare State, thus substituting a compulsory system for a voluntary one, Gladstone's Christian State without the Christian; its goods so hideous as to bring about an altogether impossible Arts and Crafts Revival; its imperialism so xenophobic as to produce two world wars and destroy five empires; its population so swollen that contraceptives are now a gilt-edged security; its black cities so frightful as to produce the most rigid planning laws in history; its mechanical genius such that the internal combustion engine is now destroying the culture from which it was born; its architecture so absurdly romantic as to produce a functionalism almost as silly.

The values have been reversed all right. If the Middle Ages were 'a prolonged penance for the sins of the Roman Empire', then the twentieth century bears the same relationship to the nineteenth. Almost everything in modern life and architecture has been either a deliberate reversal of some nineteenth-century value, or a solution of some problem which, without the nineteenth century, would never have existed.

We have reversed the Victorian values, but we live all the time in a continuation of the Victorian Age. One cannot be born on to a virgin planet; therein lies the falsity of all the hygienic utopias. One by one the Wellsian fantasies are coming true; we hardly recognize them because they are coming true in a mainly Victorian setting. The hang-overs are always tremendous. Elizabethan mansions were just

Perpendicular churches with flat ceilings; Classic Revival town-halls were just bits of intellectual snobbery for the benefit of places like Liverpool or Birmingham; while our own society is riddled through and through, every moment of our lives, with Victorian nostalgias.

Therein, for us, lies the fascination of the Victorian Age – its manners, its taste, its art and architecture. We have repudiated it and yet, whether we like it or not, we are part of it. It explains us to ourselves. As we look back through this story of Victorian architecture we see each chapter, not only as a story in itself, but also – however transmuted – as something bearing upon today.

Some would name the Industrial Revolution itself as having altered our world, cities and buildings, more than any other single thing. Certainly it is the Industrial Revolution that has borne us along the road from that old Georgian agricultural England to the England that we know now. Certainly, as we mark off the industrial achievements of our grandfathers – bridges, stations, factories, first in iron and then in steel or concrete – the story continues without a break into our own time. From that first iron bridge at Coalbrookdale to the new Forth Road Bridge, it is one process. From the iron roof over Euston Station to Nervi's Olympic Stadium in Rome is one process. The reason the work of the Victorian engineers – 'the Railway Age' – has been so popularized is only partly nostalgia; mainly it is because it is all thought of as the 'pre-history' of modern architecture.

132 Boat Shed, Sheerness. *The sort of anonymous design which represents so well the 'functional tradition'. This was never intended to be 'architectural' and so – like, say, the Roman aqueducts – it succeeds in being architecture of a high order.*

But that is only part of the truth. For one thing the very magnitude of that industrial, scientific and mechanical achievement has taken us clean out of that Victorian 'paleotcchnic' era of coal and iron, into our own 'neotechnic' era of electricity and petrol, moving the centre of gravity of a nation from the coalfields of the North to the suburbia of the South-East.

For another thing, industrialism and engineering were not the only antecedents of modernism ... perhaps not even the main ones. Our culture is as fragmented as ever ... in City banks and 'civic centres' and in commercialized elegance, High Victorianism still spawns its children; they may not be so very like their parents, but there is still an architecture of the Establishment. Moreover, if modern architecture has, at least in outward form, repudiated the Gothic Revival it is still, whether it knows it or not, highly romantic. The medievalism may have gone but the romanticism has not. Modern architecture, in all its outward forms, has repudiated all the Gothic forms – indeed it was in itself a revolt against historic styles – but there is still a lot of romanticism and nostalgia interwoven with the formalism. It is not only that a great pile such as Liverpool's Anglican cathedral is still building. It is doing so side by side with a Catholic cathedral which a medieval master-mason – in command of reinforced concrete and on an off-day – might have been tempted to build. Coventry – with its long vista, tall windows, high vault and slender columns – is about as Gothic as a 'modern' building can be. And Le Corbusier's pilgrim church at Ronchamp has all the naïve charm and solemnity of some tenth-century Balkan chapel.

The Gothic Revival, indeed, so penetrated Victorian thought that it is taking more than steel and concrete to get it out of our system. If, in his reaction to the mass-produced horrors of the 1851 Exhibition, William Morris saw hope only in his hopelessly idealized medieval world, while others, in the Crystal Palace itself, saw the dawn of a new architecture, then it may be said that neither side has triumphed. The 'modern movement' has consisted largely in bringing those two warring elements to terms with each other.

The Arts and Crafts Movement, in concentrating upon 'craftsmanship' was really, although it would never have admitted it, on the side of the engineers; in its exclusive concern with wood and stone and its hatred of the machine, it was still on the side of medievalism. Voysey, as has been said, has often been considered a prophet of modernism and of functionalism. In fact he lived long enough to hate all modern architecture; he used those plain square mullions only because there were no medieval craftsmen to carve them; while the very use of mullions in any shape or form was, of course, in itself a piece of medievalism. (Had not Pugin, almost a century earlier, remarked after a visit to Oxford: 'How strange to find such a glorious man as Ward living in a room without mullions!'?) As for Mackintosh, in the Glasgow Art School he thought he was designing in a new style, whereas actually, of course, neither his *Art Nouveau* twirls nor his big 'engineer's' windows can disguise the fact that the total building – more even than anything that, say, Butterfield or Pugin might have built – would have been approved by the master-masons of Chartres.

Now that was just the kind of thinking that William Morris had never arrived at ... let alone Ruskin. They were both born too soon. Morris, having set workmanship and the workman upon a high pinnacle, became a founding father of Socialism, believing that through political action he might give back to the workman all that he had lost at the end of the Middle Ages. It was a starry-eyed belief, and Morris soon found that he had to train a very few experts to imitate a style and to revive techniques which truly had no place in the nineteenth century. That is why despite Walter Gropius's very real admiration for Morris, the story which Professor Pevsner calls 'From William Morris to Walter Gropius' is really the story of a revolution. That revolution took us from a hatred of the machine that was almost virulent to a use of the machine that was intelligent. Only when that revolution had been completed could we say that the Gothic Revival was behind us.

Walter Gropius (b. 1883) is not, in the ordinary sense, among the greatest of modern architects. His place is a different one. Le Corbusier, having altered our whole conception of how men should live in cities, has been a more dramatic, more obvious influence than Gropius. Lloyd Wright, having harnessed all the forces of the romantic movement to the new age, has struck men's imagination more than Gropius. Mies van der Rohe – with those chaste essays in glass and steel – has married the three elements of a 'total architecture' – function, beauty

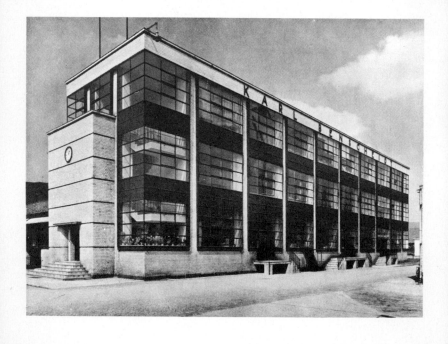

and structure – thus hinting that we may be in the dawn of some new and highly architectural epoch.

Gropius has been more down to earth. He has been the catalyst, one of the forces that has carried us from the nineteenth century to the twentieth. Thanks to Gropius, every good chair, every telephone, every light-fitting and typewriter, is better than it might have been and so is the whole of American architectural education.

Full industrialism came late in Germany. Free industrial enterprise had come to France with the Revolution. By the early nineteenth century England was well on the way to being the first fully industrialized state in history. In Germany such freedom was not permitted until the sixties. The flowering of romanticism, the romanticism of Weimar, preceded rather than accompanied industrialization; it was not until the seventies that the full flood of industrialism swept across Germany, wiping out cottage industries and craftsmen.

It was on this high tide that Gropius was born in 1883. In 1911 he designed the Fagus Factory, at Alfeld in North Germany – a significant landmark in the story of modern architecture – and at that date a work of genius. Peter Behrens, in his famous Berlin Turbine Hall (1909) [133] had already conceived an industrial architecture of glass and steel, but whereas Behrens's large windows were tied between pylons of massive masonry, Gropius created a new art form. He set back the supporting columns from the face of the glass, cantilevering out the floors and thus, in effect, abolishing the wall – for thousands of years the basis of architecture.

The Fagus Factory [134] rivals Sullivan's and Wright's Chicago buildings for the title of 'the first modern building'. It was designed at a time of tremendous intellectual activity in Germany. Van der Velde, although Belgian, was working in Berlin and exhibiting his furniture in Dresden. French Impressionist paintings were being shown in the National Gallery in Berlin, while a Museum of Modern Art had been founded at Hagen in the Rhineland. The German *Werkbund* was founded in Munich in 1907; its aim was 'to raise the standard of manufactured products by the joint efforts of art, industry and craftsmanship'. The *Werkbund* Year Book of 1913 contained an article by Gropius where he speaks of the 'unacknowledged majesty of American grain silos', adding that they can stand comparison with the buildings of ancient Egypt. In 1913 such statements were almost shocking.

By 1918, in the fervid, hot-house atmosphere of post-war Germany, Walter Gropius worked on a new project for art education, combining the Weimar Academy with the School of Arts and Crafts. The result was the Bauhaus. Every student had two teachers for each subject – an artist and a master-craftsman. This was at a time when students in English art schools were still doing carefully shaded drawings from antique casts, while in schools of architecture they were doing meticulous drawings of the classical 'orders'.

This first Bauhaus was doomed. Nowhere but in post-war Germany would Gropius have been allowed to launch the scheme at all; nowhere else would there have been such violent opposition. The Bauhaus became the symbol of the clash between a new and emancipated Germany on the other hand, and the old *bourgeois* and Kaiserin Germany on the other hand. The influence of Cubism, Dadaism and Expressionism upon the early Bauhaus was undeniable, and it met with disapproval. For Gropius to gather round him on his staff such derided outcasts as Paul Klee, Marcel Breuer, Kandinsky or Moholy-Nagy was almost madness. All this, despite the historical continuity of our story, was now a million miles from Morris, Arts and Crafts and *Das Englisch Haus*. The whispering began and it was not altogether unlike the shrieks of Dr Goebbels twenty years later.

In 1926 the Bauhaus left Weimar for Dessau where it had some support from local industry. There, too, Gropius made another major contribution to the modern movement. He built the Bauhaus itself. It was a remarkable achievement. It was a complex of buildings – workshops, hostels, offices and auditorium. It was efficient and functional. Like the Fagus Factory, the new Bauhaus used the glass wall, but the whole concept was now rationalized. What matters, however, is not so much Gropius as an architect, but Gropius as an influence and as a teacher – in short, what matters is the Bauhaus as an idea.

What was that idea? In essence it was this. William Morris had repudiated the machine and, in theory and in practice, done everything to restore the Medieval status of the craftsman. That was the dream, but the industrial world, like a Juggernaut, went on its way. Gropius accepted the machine, glorying in its potentialities, but

accepting it only in order to understand, to tame it and civilize it. The machine, after all, was only an extension of the hand, an elaborate tool. Man was still the master. The Machine was something one must design *for*, not something one must design *against*. On those terms the craftsman might be brought back into the industrialized world of the twentieth century. That, at least, was both the idea and the ideal of the Bauhaus.

Here we have the first hint of something which, by the middle of the twentieth century, was running through most design and almost all architecture ... the designer as a member of a 'team'. The sheer complexity of a highly technological society, with complex processes underlying the simplest object and the largest building, made some such conception of the designer's role inevitable ... perhaps a necessity. A necessity, however, is not in itself a gain. Whether the idea of a designer as a contributor, rather than as a sole conceiver, is consistent with the high position which the previous century had been trying to give to the supremacy of the imagination as a divine act – is something which, today, is still not clear. We may well ask whether or not the multiplication of the single artist into a 'team' of technicians is not, for good or ill, at least as fundamental as the invention of the machine itself. There, somewhere, in the absence of the single artist–designer–maker, may lie the so-called 'soulless' nature of much present-day architecture and industrial design ... even if, technically, it has a smooth perfection that is above criticism.

The Bauhaus was an international force – the greatest single force in the field of design between the two world wars. It was never specifically a school of architecture, but since everything had to be part of a whole, architecture was never far away. In well-equipped workshops – now a commonplace in colleges of technology – the Bauhaus taught product design, furniture, fabrics, silverware, vehicle design and pottery, typography, painting, advertising, photography, films, drama and ballet. Here and there, as in the wood furniture, there was still a ghost of Morris; here and there, as in the use of a cog-wheel motif in decoration, the machine-age was too obviously emphasized; here and there was more than a touch of *Art Nouveau*, of Cubism or Constructivism. The Bauhaus was self-conscious and inbred, but its ideas endured. It was a genuine attempt to subordinate design to the machine and to new materials, as for centuries it had been subordinated to the tool and to wood and stone. In its short crisis-ridden career – before it was finally closed to forestall a more forcible closure by the Nazis – the Bauhaus trained some five hundred men and women. It influenced all Europe. After Gropius, as a refugee, had in 1937 accepted the Chair of Architecture at Harvard, it influenced all America too.

The Bauhaus, therefore, whether directly or indirectly, was a major force in leading the twentieth-century designer out of the Victorian world into the world we know. Victorianism had symbolized a great conflict – the romantic imagination versus the machine. For good or ill, it had been Walter Gropius's task to resolve that conflict.

The nineteenth century had been England's century. England had been 'top nation', workshop of the world, the great *Herrenvolk*. Whether in romantic Gothic or engineering England had been the pace setter. It is, therefore, significant that as the Victorian Age draws to a close, the two figures who mark the transition to our own time are, respectively, Central European and American – Walter Gropius and Frank Lloyd Wright (1869–1958).

It was sometime in the eighties that Walt Whitman (1819–92) wrote in 'Specimen Days' about the Prairies and the Great Plains.

I could not help thinking [he wrote], that it would be grander still to see all those inimitable American areas fused in the alembic of a perfect poem, or other aesthetic work, entirely western, fresh and limitless – altogether our own, without a taste or trace of Europe's soil, reminiscence, technical letter or spirit.

At the turn of the century the American cultural scene may have been disastrous, but it was also pregnant. Outwardly it was either materialistic and philistine, or else it was intellectually and snobbishly bastard-European. The two poles of that world were Chicago and Boston – the Chicago of the meat-packers and the Boston of Henry James. It was, superficially, the same dichotomy as the England of the Railway boom set against the England of Oxford and the country houses ... but only superficially and outwardly. It had one enormous advantage. It was not so irrevocably chained to the past; it was tremendously virile.

In architecture that dross of the European tradition was embodied in the official American worship of the École des Beaux Arts, and of the least inspired sort of English neo-Gothic. These two kinds of architectural thinking are found at their most facile, most professional, but also most esoteric, in the work of a firm such as McKim, Mead and White (Pennsylvania Station, New York, 1906; Municipal Building, New York, 1910) or the work of such a man as Bertram Goodhue (1869–1924) and many of the same kind. Their collegiate Gothic is to be seen on almost every American campus.

The final liberation of the young American architect from an École des Beaux Arts training – whether in Paris or in one of the many sham écoles of the American universities – was not really complete until 1937, the year of Gropius's arrival in Harvard. Perhaps, anyway, it was only out in the Middle West – over against the little brick-box houses of the prairies, or in response to the fine uninhibited vulgarity of Chicago, that a new architecture could be born ... that, in Walt Whitman's words, 'a Child came forth'.

Louis Sullivan (1856–1924) was born in Boston, but worked and died in Chicago. Everyone thinks of him as the man who 'invented' the skyscraper, with the young Frank Lloyd Wright at his elbow. That is an oversimplified picture, but it is in fact an example – and there are many in history – of how economic pressures, land values, may make imperious demands upon architecture ... only to find an imaginative as well as a technical response. Sullivan himself has told of the 'break-through', of how, almost overnight, he had the idea of hanging the stone on the steel ... and a whole new architectural world opened before him.

But if Sullivan is known to history as the architect of the Chicago Auditorium Building (1887) [137], the Wainwright Building (1890) or the Carson Pirie Scott Store (1899 and 1902) [138], and half-a-dozen other remarkable monuments of that decade – each more fundamentally 'modern' than are most buildings sixty years later – he is less well-known as a poet and a philosopher. Sullivan, although apparently the first architect of modern materialism, shows in his work continuity as well as transformation – what he called the 'idealism of transcendentalism'. Like the English romantic poets he saw Man's creative

power as the link with the Divine – the act Man shares with God. Sullivan's God, in the last analysis is, like Lloyd Wright's, the pantheistic one of Wordsworth and Whitman. And if Sullivan is linked, in this respect, with the Romantics, he must also be linked with, say, Grant Allen, Havelock Ellis or Wynwood Reade, a whole group of prophetic figures who, like Sullivan, await revaluation. Sullivan was, not only architecturally but philosophically, the very necessary forerunner of Frank Lloyd Wright.

Frank Lloyd Wright was the arch-romantic, the seer and the prophet of the new America. In a long, dramatic and very flamboyant life – punctuated by murder, arson, rape and sudden death – he managed to create new values for a nation – partly by the demolition of old values, but partly by the sublimation of old ones. His colleagues disliked his arrogance, but if the creative artist believes that the creative act is shared with God, then, as Lloyd Wright said, he has 'a basis for his arrogance'. It was only before his master, Sullivan, before Whitman, Ruskin and the great English romantics, that Lloyd Wright could bow his head in humility.

He was an eccentric, in the great line of English eccentrics who decided, one hundred and fifty years ago, that the Age of Reason was so reasonable that human nature could bear it no longer. And so this very 'modern' architect found himself – rather curiously – a latter-day figure of the Romantic Movement. He liked quoting the passage from Victor Hugo, significantly suppressed by the French Academy, that the Renaissance was a great sunset that the world had mistaken for a great dawn. He looked back to Carlyle's *Past and Present*, with its emphasis upon the communal efficiency of the good Medieval life; he looked back to Walt Whitman and to Ruskin for their adoration of Nature; to Shelley and Samuel Butler and Kropotkin for their personal revolt in the cause of freedom; to Tolstoy for his belief in the real Jesus; to Morris and Lethaby for their aesthetic socialism and honest craftsmanship.

Lloyd Wright, however, more than any of the puritanical Victorians, knew that an artist must also have a sensual joy in things. That was his addition to the total picture we have tried to build up. When he saw real evil he could himself become the high moralizing puritan and would then defy every convention of a puritan society.

He had the dark, unabashed sexual passion of the Victorian patriarchs, all mixed up with an adoration, also passionate, of stars in the Arizona night or of almond blossom against the sky.

Lloyd Wright's medium happened to be architecture. He thus found himself a romantic architect, a traditionalist in a land without traditions. His opposite numbers in England – Lutyens, for instance, who was born the same year – were using their expertise in adapting a sham vernacular for the use of a sham aristocracy, in handling traditions so strong as to suffocate real design. Lloyd Wright, on the other hand, having no precedents at all, had to ask himself some very basic questions about the real nature of architecture. In the end he discovered his own tradition, or rather its equivalent. He found it in the soil, in the landscape, in an 'organic architecture' that grows out of the site and out of the problem. He discovered it in the basic American qualities of pine, granite and rock, or in the brilliance of the painted desert – all cacti and golden stone – out in the sun beyond Phoenix.

Steeped in the romantic past, and under the guiding star of Whitman and Emerson, both Sullivan and Wright marched, as it were, into the West, in the wake of the covered wagons, clear-eyed and uninhibited, leaving a false culture behind them. They worshipped Nature and Man, but never for one moment fell to the temptation of scorning their own epoch. If the forest and the prairies were the temple where they worshipped, they never repudiated the ugly, urban, seething culture of Chicago and New York. That was life, and as architects, therefore, it was something they must come to terms with. Wright's genius lay in the consummation of a marriage between, on the one hand, that ethos of the forest and camp fire and, on the other hand, that full acceptance of the machine and the great city. Whitman himself, after all, as he lay on his berth on the Santa Fé express, had – even before Kipling – hymned the railroad and the electric telegraph, and all that they implied. That reconciliation of the forest and the city may be said to summarize Lloyd Wright's America, as well as his own major contribution to architectural theory.

A quarter of a century before either the Bauhaus or the English MARS Group was founded, Lloyd Wright recognized that the artist, if he was to survive, must both preserve his imagination, and enter into

some kind of partnership with the scientist. Otherwise he is an anachronism 'doomed to patronage by rich and culture-curious *entre-preneurs*'. This was something which Morris had tried to face at the end of his life but could never quite swallow. It was the mainspring of Lloyd Wright's work. If his finest houses are only a kind of million-aire's sublimation of the log cabin, he was also the first man to grasp the implications of a framed architecture derived from steel. In 1891, at the Wainwright Building in Buffalo, Sullivan had built the first steel-framed structure; in 1906, at Oak Hill Park, Ohio, Lloyd Wright had conceived a church which was the first reinforced concrete mono-lith. 'The trick was turned,' said Sullivan, 'and then swiftly came into being something new under the sun.'

The intrinsic faults of Lloyd Wright's work are not hard to find. They are not important. Perhaps it was the large sweep of a philo-sophical mind, the adoration of the big things in Nature, that explain his insensitivity to ornament. Sullivan, in a curiously rich version of *Art Nouveau* gave us, here and there, a brilliant *tour-de-force* in cast iron sheathing. Lloyd Wright, one suspects, was not interested and so – in ornament – produced very little more than a very odd blend of *Art Nouveau* and pseudo-Aztec. That may have been just a doomed attempt to discover a system of ornament indigenous to America – which didn't need one – or it may have been the inevitable by-product of stripping romantic architecture of its Gothic clothing – a filling of the vacuum. More likely it was that the young Lloyd Wright was still living within the shadow of an age that had equated 'architecture' with 'ornamented building'. Anyway, in the end, Lloyd Wright's best work was organic, derived from the site and from structure and from vision ... with no ornament whatsoever.

In Lloyd Wright's work, however, there might easily have been a more disastrous dichotomy. The native house, all granite, pine and open hearth – his 'organic' architecture – might well have proved utterly irreconcilable with the new architecture of steel or concrete. In the event this was not so. The two emerge as a single thing, a style – a reconciliation of apparent opposites, of the organic–romantic and the technical. It was in this way that Sullivan and Wright gave back to Europe a great theory of architecture. The techniques were new techniques; the theory was the theory of Gothic. It was the marriage

of the potential of the machine with that high romanticism which, as we have seen, had been built up steadily throughout the nineteenth century.

The famous Oak Hill Park Unity Church was, to be honest, a trifle Egyptological, consciously stylistic; but still it *was* reinforced concrete, and it did – in 1906 – have the 'services', heating and so on, built into the structure. Significantly, although the more 'modern' building of the two, it preceded the Robie House (1909) by three years. This later house had a great central chimney stack, with hearth to match, long low lines and an almost cyclopaean or primeval aspect. It hugged the ground and it was both spacious and strong. It also, in its deft handling of space, foreshadowed the present day 'open plan'. For all its rugged domesticity, however, it also exploited the inherent possibilities of the cantilever in concrete – those long deep shadows are the product of big overhangs and big span beams. A quarter of a century later, at Falling Waters, Bear Run, in the Kaufmann House (1936) Lloyd Wright built an American home in a birch forest. It hangs over a waterfall. Each room, each terrace of that house, is a concrete shelf projecting, unsupported, far out over the crags of the cataracts. It is perhaps a 'folly' of a sort, but aesthetically the horizontal shelves are the foil to the vertical tree trunks, while the whole thing is a most vivid symbol of those two architectures – the organic and the technical. If the young Lloyd Wright first discovered himself in the Chicago of the nineties, he found himself aligned, by the middle of this century – whether he approved of them or not – with such younger masters as Robert Maillart, the Swiss designer of bridges, as Pier Luigi Nervi, the Italian engineer, or as Le Corbusier.

Chicago and Lloyd Wright acted in the end as a kind of catharsis upon European architecture. Europe, in the years before and after the First World War, was so inhibited and hidebound by her stylistic habits – every European city proclaims the fact – that the catharsis, when it came, was all the greater. In France, it is true, the École des Beaux Arts has never acknowledged the existence of the world it lives in, but in the event this has only served to dramatize the isolation and singularity of Le Corbusier. In England – although England had been the real womb of the modern movement – the old nineteenth-century 'Battle of the Styles' was a skirmish compared with this new battle of the Modern Movement – a battle for the mere recognition that such a thing as 'modern architecture' could exist at all.

England's insular immunity to external influences – or, rather, her own very peculiar response to those influences – led the world to believe that England was outside the modern movement altogether. Sigfried Giedion, writing of that movement in Germany, and of the Bauhaus in particular, remarked that during the first quarter of this century, 'England had slept'. This was not really true. After all, the country of both the Arts and Crafts Movement and of 'the Railway Age' was bound, somehow or other, to play a part in the making of an architecture which was virtually a fusion of those two things. If the German Gropius and the American Lloyd Wright were the midwives, Victorian England had been the womb.

It was Victorian England that had seen the disastrous divorce between architect and engineer, and it was true, therefore, that it was in England that the healing of the breach was most difficult – each side holding the other in contempt. The Victorian architect had tried to turn himself into a professional gentleman, while the engineer was stealing the big contracts – to the ultimate degradation of both.

Nevertheless that divorce and an eventual reconciliation – the reconciliation of imagination and technique – are in effect what modern architecture and design are all about. That reconciliation the Victorian Age, with all its virtues, had never discovered. It is a reconciliation that the twentieth century, with all its defects, must discover if its arts are to survive.

Bibliography

This bibliography could have been much longer. I have excluded articles and published lectures, such as have appeared in the *Transactions of the RIBA* or the professional journals during the last hundred and fifty years. Many references to these will be found in some of the books in the list below. I have, necessarily, excluded the vast mass of Victorian literature which does not deal directly with architecture although it might amplify the picture of the Age. I have also excluded books on foreign architecture unless they have been referred to in the text.

GENERAL BOOKS

Boase, T.S.R., *English Art 1800–1870* [1959]
Architecture cannot be understood without an understanding of the other arts. This book is valuable in itself and for its bibliography.

Carlyle, Thomas, *Past and Present* [1843]
Past and Present, although not touching directly upon architecture, did open the eyes of a whole generation to the fact that the Middle Ages were something more than merely picturesque. Much praised by William Morris.

Casson, H., *An Introduction to Victorian Architecture* [1948]
Exactly what it purports to be.

Clark, Kenneth, *The Gothic Revival* [1950]
First published in 1928, revised in its present edition, this book was virtually this century's 'rediscovery' of an important phase of Victorian architecture then still in eclipse.

Clarke, B.F.L., *Church Builders of the Nineteenth Century* [1938]
Useful for factual information.

Eastlake, C.L., *A History of the Gothic Revival* [1872]
Interesting to compare this Victorian account with Kenneth Clark's, written more than half a century later.

Ellis, Hamilton, *British Railway History 1830–1874* [1954]
A good 'background' to the work of the engineers; also a good picture of ruthless individualism.

Fergusson, J., *History of Architecture* (3 vols.) [1869]. *Volume III: The Modern Styles*
A Victorian account, in a well-known general history of what was then 'modern'.

Ferriday (Ed.), *Victorian Architecture* [1963]
A symposium of good essays on aspects of Victorian architecture, and upon most of the greater English architects of the nineteenth century. Well illustrated.

Fitch, J. M., *American Architecture: The Forces That Shape It* [1948]
An explanation, among other things, of how American and English architecture gradually differed more and more from each other.

Goodhart-Rendel, H. S., *English Architecture Since the Regency* [1953]
A brilliant and erudite, if sometimes rather wrong-headed, account of some of the more obscure Victorian architects.

Gropius, W., *New Architecture and the Bauhaus* [1936] ￼
The 'bible' of the first conscious and formulated protest against the whole Victorian attitude to form and taste.

Hitchcock, H.-R., *Early Victorian Architecture in Britain* (2 vols.) [1954]
An excellent and well illustrated book.
            Architecture: Nineteenth and Twentieth Centuries [1958]
Although dealing with a much wider field than that of Victorian architecture, this is a massive compendium of facts.

Hussey, C., *The Picturesque* [1927]
A good book on a subject which is, strictly, pre-Victorian, but essential to its understanding.

Kerr, R., *The Gentleman's House* [1869]
A text-book for the successful Victorian architect with a flourishing and upper middle-class domestic practice.

Le Corbusier, *Vers Une Architecture* (*Towards a New Architecture*) [1927]
Although not so intended, this famous book was perhaps the most pungent, if belated, comment upon the architecture of the nineteenth century.

Lethaby, W., *Architecture* [1911]
            Form in Civilization [1922]
The first realization that architecture had something to do with life as well as with art. *Architecture*, in 'The Home University Library' became a classic and has been re-issued.

Lilley, S., *Men, Machines and History* [1948]
A most useful addendum to the whole story of Victorian industrialism and functional architecture.

Madsen, S. T., *Sources of Art Nouveau* [1956]
Useful as a sort of supplement to Howarth's monograph on Mackintosh, q.v.

March Phillipps, L., *Works of Man* [1913]
          Form and Colour [1915]
Like Lethaby, March Phillipps saw architecture as something far more than style –
born of climate, geology and of life – thus transcending the Victorian conception.

Morris, William, *Hopes and Fears for Art*, and *Lectures on Art and Industry*
          (Volume XXII in *Collected Works*) [1910]
Everything Morris wrote is to some extent necessary to a complete understanding
of the greatest single break in the complacent continuity of the Victorian Age;
this volume deals more directly with architecture; the romances do so only by
implication.

Mumford, L., *The Brown Decades* [1931]
A most brilliant analysis of the social background of mid-Victorian America, and
the consequences for cities and for architecture.

Pevsner, N., *Pioneers of Modern Design* [1949]
The greatest single work, a classic, on the subject of its sub-title – 'William Morris
to Walter Gropius'.
          Outline of European Architecture [1957]
Our subject is only a small part of this large work, but the book – for those who
need a general introduction to architecture, is probably the best available.

Ruskin, John, *Seven Lamps of Architecture* [1849]
          Stones of Venice (3 vols.) [1851–3]
          Unto This Last [1862]
The library edition of the works of John Ruskin runs to thirty-nine volumes.
These three books are the ones which, more than the others, influenced architec-
tural taste and thought.

Pugin, A.W.N., *Contrasts* [1836]
          True Principles of Christian Architecture [1841]
          Apology for the Revival of Christian Architecture in England [1843]
Pugin's written works, illustrated by himself, were virtually propaganda broad-
sheets of a virulent kind in favour of the Gothic Revival. They show the tremendous moral indignation called up in Victorian breasts by the issue of 'style'.

Sullivan, L.H., *The Autobiography of an Idea* [1949]
Sullivan's highly personal account of his life and of how under his inspiration, and
then Lloyd Wright's, the 'Chicago school' came into being.

Summerson, John, *Heavenly Mansions* [1949]
A collection of essays of which the one on Butterfield entitled 'The Glory of
Ugliness' is outstanding.

Young, G.M. (Ed.), *Early Victorian England* (2 vols.) [1934]
The classic account of all aspects of life in England from 1830 to 1865. Professor
A.E.Richardson's chapter on 'Architecture' is good, but others such as 'Homes
and Habits' and 'Town Life' have a bearing on our subject.

MONOGRAPHS

Barry, A., *Life and Works of Sir Charles Barry* [1867]
This is the 'official' life of Barry, by his son. As such it is authoritative, but filial piety has prevented justice being done to Pugin over the respective parts which he and Barry played in the building of the Houses of Parliament.

Scott-Moncrieff, W., *John Francis Bentley* [1924]
The life and work of the architect of the Roman Catholic cathedral at Westminster.

Pullan, A., *Architectural Designs of William Burges* (2 vols.) [1887]

Harbron, D., *The Conscious Stone: The Life of Edward William Godwin* [1942]
A fascinating book. The life of the man who became Ellen Terry's husband, and was by no means the least of the *Art Nouveau* architects – second perhaps only to Mackintosh.

Giedion, S., *Walter Gropius* [1954]
A good life of Gropius has still to be written. This is at least authoritative on the Bauhaus period.

Howarth, Thomas, *C. Rennie Mackintosh and the Modern Movement* [1952]
A first-rate definitive life of Mackintosh, and of the movement of which he was the leader. Unlikely to be superseded.

Mackail, J. W., *Life of William Morris* [1922]
Since Mackail wrote this book there have been several books on Morris; this is still the authoritative one in that it was written by someone who knew him well. It 'plays down' Morris's socialism, but is otherwise good.

Morris, May, *The Art of William Morris* [1936]
Uniform with the Collected Works, this 'life' by Morris's daughter is well worth-while. There is a companion volume on *Morris as a Socialist*, with a preface by Bernard Shaw.

Summerson, John, *John Nash* [1935]
As a preliminary to a study of Victorian architecture, some understanding of the Regency is essential; this book is as helpful as any.

Markham, Violet, *Paxton and the Bachelor Duke* [1935]
Written by his grand-daughter, this life of Paxton, designer of the Crystal Palace and Head Gardener to the Duke of Devonshire, is both authoritative and entertaining.

Chadwick, George F., *Works of Sir Joseph Paxton* [1961]
This book on Paxton is rather more serious than Miss Markham's. It shows what an astonishing amount of architectural work was done by Paxton, in addition to the things for which he has always been famous. He emerges as a town-planner and architect, as well as horticulturist and engineer. He is also seen as the typically Victorian self-made man.

Ferrey, B., *Pugin: Recollections* [1861]
Gives the facts about Pugin's life, but was written too soon to judge fairly either the architectural or religious controversies of which Pugin was always the centre.

Trappes-Lomax, M., *Pugin, a Mediaeval Victorian* [1932]
This is a brilliant biography of one of the most fascinating and controversial figures of the whole era.

Gwyn, Denis, *Lord Shrewsbury, Pugin and the Catholic Revival* [1946]
With the Catholic Emancipation Act, and the general revival of Catholicism in England, Pugin acquired as patrons a most curious collection of rich and eccentric noblemen – Scarisbrick, Alton Towers as well as many churches and monasteries were the outcome.

Blomfield, Sir R., *Richard Norman Shaw* [1940]
A good life of a fashionable, brilliant but highly eclectic late Victorian architect.

Street, A.E., *Memoir of George Edmund Street* [1888]
A new life of G.E.Street, architect of the Law Courts and of many churches, is awaited; meanwhile this gives the facts.

Gibb, A., *Life of Thomas Telford* [1935]
A good life of a pioneer engineer.

Hitchcock, H.-R., *Frank Lloyd Wright: In The Nature of Materials* [New York, 1942]
Frank Lloyd Wright attracts authors and the books about him are legion. Not one of them is entirely satisfactory. This is probably the best.

Farr, Finis, *Frank Lloyd Wright* [1962]
This is a sensational and, indeed, journalistic, account of Lloyd Wright's sensational life. It concentrates upon sex and disaster rather than upon the architecture of the master. That it is highly readable cannot be denied.

Wright, Frank Lloyd, *Autobiography* [1942]
Wright has not done himself much more justice than his numerous biographers. All the same – another readable book, even if crammed with self-justification that is unnecessary, and with sentiment that is embarrassing.

Pevsner, N., *Matthew Digby Wyatt* [1950]
A good life of the last of the Wyatts – the one who designed Alford House, off Kensington Gore, and who cooperated with Brunel in the design of Paddington Station.

Note: Most of the books in this list have their own bibliographies which show where the subject can be followed up in greater detail.

Index

Numerals in italics refer to illustrations

Adam, Robert, 39, 68, 72, 211
Adam, Robert, *et al.*; Strawberry Hill, *64, 65*
Adler, Dankmar, *254, 259*
Admiralty Arch, London, *146*, 164
A.E.G. Turbine factory, Berlin, *245*, 247
Age of Reason, 42, 255
Albert, Prince, 92, 126, 128, 153, 159, *212*, 214
Albert Hall, London, 93
Albert Memorial, London, 92–4, *95, 106*, 137, 158
Alberti, L. B., 58, 60, 186
Alford House, Kensington, *212*
All Saints, Margaret Street, London, *88*, 89–90, 137
All Saints, Stand, Lancs., 72
Allen, Grant, 255
Alma-Tadema, L., 185
Alton Towers, Staffs., 81, *83*, 84, 208, 213
Ancient Mariner, The (Coleridge), 48
Angelico, Fra, 172
Apology for the revival of Christian Architecture in England (Pugin), *77*
Architect and Patronage, 206–9, 224–6
Architecture, a Profession or an Art (Morris *et al.*), 186
Architecture of the Nineteenth and Twentieth Centuries (Hitchcock), 15
Arcuated, 131
Art and Craft of the Machine (Wright), 184
Art Nouveau, 164, 187, 189, 192–203, *194, 195, 196*, 232, 234, 250, 258
Arts and Crafts Movement, 105, 164, 178, 186–90, 191, 201, 232, 241, 243, 248, 261

Arundel, Sussex, 68
Ashridge Castle, Herts., 71, 211
Assize Court, Manchester, *158*
Athenaeum, London, 143
Attempt to discriminate styles of English Architecture (Rickman), 136
Auditorium Building, Chicago, 252, *254*

Bacon, Francis, 63
Badminton, Glos., 238
Baillie Scott, M.H., 190, 192, 219, 234
Balmoral, Castle, 214, *215*
Bagehot, Walter, 111
Baker, Herbert, *146*, 230
Banbury Road, Oxford (No. 81), *236*
Bank of England, Liverpool, *145*, 147
Bank of England, London, 74, 152
Banqueting House, Whitehall, 19
Barlow, W.H., 94, *128*
Barry, Sir Charles, 19, 72, 74, 75, *75*, 77, *84*, 84–5, *85, 86, 87*, 92, 97, 98, 137, 138, 143, 153, 164, 208, 209, 215–19, *221*, 224, 226; and Pugin, 84–5, *84, 85, 87*
Bath, 16, 34, 46, 50, 63
Batty Langley, 66
Bauhaus, 178, 248–51, 256
Bazalgette, V., *122*
Beardsley, Aubrey, 197, 198, 203
Beata Beatrix, 45, 198
Beckford, William, 42, 45, 71, 72, 79, 206, 209–10
Beggerstaff, J. and W., 197
Behrens, Peter, *245*, 247
Belle Dame sans merci, La, 198
Belvoir Castle, Leics., 68, *69*, 136, 211
Bentley, Richard, Illustrator to Gray, *67*, 68

269

Berlin, A.E.G. Turbine Factory, *245*, 247
Bessemer, H., 28, 35
Bethnal Green model dwellings, 239
Betjeman, John, 15, 16
Birkbeck Bank, Chancery Lane, *22*
Birmingham, 19, 31, 34, 40, 242; Law Courts, 164; St Chad's Cathedral, 81, *82*; Temple of Jupiter Stator, 152; University, 164
Blaise, nr Bristol, *54*, 55, 238
Blake, William, 46, 47
Blenheim, Oxon, 61, 210
Bloomfield, R., 232
Blore, Edward, *et al.*, *220*
Boat Shed, Sheerness, Kent, *242*
Bodley, G.F., 105, *108*
Bohemian, 42, 148, 187, 208
Boileau, L.H., 131, 187
Borromini, F., 69
Bourneville, 55, 237, *238*
Brasenose College, Oxford, *107*
Breuer, Marcel, 248
Brighton: Metropole Hotel, *154*; Pavilion, 208; St Peter's, 72
Bridgewater House, London, 216, 219
Bristol, 26; Temple Meads Station, 118
Britannia Bridge, Menai Strait, *118*
British Museum, London, 74, 143, *144*, 147
Broadley's, Lake Windermere, 190
Brodrick, Cuthbert, 152, *154*, *156*
Brompton Oratory, Kensington, 78, *163*
Brontë, Emily, 46
Brown, 'Capability' Lancelot, 52
Brown, Ford Madox, *112*, 113
Browning, R. and E.B., 40, 46, 209
Brunel, I.K., 29, 30, 35, *36*, *37*, 118, 128, 131, 148
Brunelleschi, F., 58, 59, 186
Bryanstone, Blandford, Dorset, 225, *232*, 232–3
Buckingham Palace, London, *53*, 164; The Bow Library, 220
Bunning, J.B., 131, *133*, 187
Burdett-Coutts, Baroness, 239
Burges, William, 100–5, *103*, *104*, 224
Burne-Jones, E., 105, 185

Burton, Decimus, *127*, 143
Bute, Marquis of, 102, 103, 224
Butler, Samuel, 255
Butterfield William, 19, 46, *88*, 89–92, *90*, *91*, 98, 102, 136, 137, 138, 148, 166, 176, 197, 244
Byron, Lord, G.G., 46, 50, 51, 71

Caernarvon, Earl of, 216
Café Royal, London, 234
Calais Beach (Turner), 46
Caledonian Road Free Church, Glasgow, *149*
Cambridge, Camden Society, 86, 89, 92, 136, 210; Downing College, 147, 148; St Johns College, 62
Cannon Street Station, London, *120*
Cardiff Castle, 102, *103*, *104*, 224
Carlisle, Lord, 207
Carlton House Terrace, London, 19, 74
Carlyle, Thomas, 46, 51, 113, 122, 178, 241, 255
Carson, Pirie, Scott Store, Chicago, 252, *257*
Castle Howard, Yorks., *207*, 210
Castle of Otranto (Walpole), 65, 210
Cenotaph, London, 235
Chambers, Sir W., 47, 68, 72, 143, 152
Charnwood Forest, Leics., 84, *188*, 188–9
Chartism, 49, 51
Chatsworth conservatory, 126, 127
Chatsworth, Estate Office, 128
Chesters, Northumberland, 232
Chicago, 27, 28, 35, 135, 184, 187, 199, 225, 230, 247, 252, 260; Auditorium Building, 252, *254*; Carson, Pirie, Scott Store, 252, *257*; Guaranty Building, *259*; Marshall Field Store, *253*; Robie House, 260
Christ Church, Oxford, 62, 65
Christ in the House of His Parents (Millais), 89
Church Building Act, 72, 74
Church Building Society, 72
Chute, 68
Cities in Evolution (Geddes), 25
City and Guilds College, S. Kensington, 162

City Chambers, Glasgow, *157*
City of London, *166*
Clark, Sir Kenneth, 15, 64, 79
Classic Revival, 74, 137–48, *149*, *150*, *151*, 242
Clifton Suspension Bridge, 131
Clivedon, Bucks., 219
Clouds, Wilts., *183*
Cloverley Hall, Salop, 226, 229
Coal Exchange, London, 131, *133*, 187
Coalbrookdale Bridge, Salop, 27, *28*, 131, 242
Cockerell, C.R., *140*, *141*, 143, *145*, 147
Colcutt, T.E., 164, *165*
Cole, Sir Henry, 159
Coleridge, S.T., 45, 46, 47–8, 55, 208
Cologne, Werkbund Exhibition factory, *249*
Colosseum, Rome, 153
Commune, 51
Comper, Ninian, 105, *109*, 178
'Compton' Chintz, *181*
Constable, John, 46
Constructivism, 250
Contrasts (Pugin), 78, 122, 178
Conway, Britannia Bridge, *118*, 123
Corbusier, Le, 19, 45, 98, 235, 243, 244, 260
Cork Cathedral, 102, 105
Cottage Ornée, 53, 55, 210
Coventry Cathedral, 243
Crace, J., 219
Cragside, Northumberland, 225, *225*
Crane, Walter, 185, 199
Cranston Tea Rooms, Ingram St, Glasgow, 201, *202*
Crossland, W. H., *217*, *218*
Crystal Palace, London, 93, 111, 113, *123*, *124*, *125*, 123–31, *129*, 135, 184, 187, 237, 243
Cubism, 248, 250
Cubitt, Lewis, *117*, *132*
Cubitt, Thomas, *117*, *212*
Cubitt, W., *117*, 159
Culzean, Scotland, 211
Cumberland Terrace, London, *139*

Dadaism, 248

Darbishire, H.A., 239
Dartmouth, Royal Naval College, 164
Darwin, Charles, 241
Das Englisch Haus (Muthesius), 178, 192, 232, 248
Davis, A.J. and Mewès, C.F., 230
Dawpool, Birkenhead, Ches., *227*
Deane, Sir Thomas, *106*, 131, *134*, 135
Deanery Garden, Sonning, 234
Decline and Fall of the Romantic Ideal (Lucas), 44
Defence of Guenevre (Morris), 177
de Morgan, William, 180
Derby, Adam, 27, *28*
Dessau, Bauhaus, 248
de Volney, Chasseboeuf, 63
Devonshire, Duke of, 55, 238
Devonshire House, London, 216
Dickens, Charles, 16, 51, 56, 122
Disraeli, B., 219
Dombey and Son (Dickens), 36, 122
Dorchester House, London, 216
Doré, Gustav, 51
Downing College, Cambridge, 147
Dream of John Ball (Morris), 177
Dresden, 247
Dromore Castle, Ireland, 234
Dunrobin Castle, Sutherland, 219, *221*

Early Victorian England (Young), 17
East Cowes, I.O.W., 211
Eastnor Castle, Hereford, 68, 136, 211
Eaton Hall, Cheshire, 136, 219, *222*, *223*
Eaton Square, London, *142*
École des Beaux Arts, 252, 260
Edensor, nr Chatsworth, 55, 238
Edinburgh High School, *150*; Prince's St, *105*, 214; Scott Memorial, 93, *105*, 214
Education Act, 39
Eiffel, Gustav, 192, 197
Eiffel Tower, 197
Eliot, George, 116
Eliot, T.S., 47
Ellerdale Road, London, Shaw's House, 229
Ellesmere, Earl of, 216
Ellis, Havelock, 255

Elmes, H.L., *140*, 143, 147, 148
Elstree, Herts., The Leys, *196*
Emerson, R., 256
English Constitution, The (Bagehot), 111
Entretiens (Viollet-le-Duc), 135
Euston Station, London, 94, 126, 128, 131, 147, *147*, 242
Evelyn, John, 52
Excursion (Wordsworth), 122
Expressionism, 248

Faber, F.W., *163*
Fagus Factory, Alfeld, *246*, 247
Falling Water, Bear Run, 260
Femme Fatale, 198 *passim*
Fielding, H., 63
First World War, 203, 260
Florence, 40, 58, 60, 186
Fonthill Abbey, Wilts., 45, *70*, 71–2, 81, 209, 213
Foreign Office, London, 74, 92, *167*
Forth Road Bridge, 242
Fowke, Francis, *162*
Frederick the Great, 50
Free Trade Hall, Manchester, 152
French Revolution, 42
Frith, W.P., *119*
Froissart, J., 62
Froude, J.A., 57
Fry, Elizabeth, 51
Functional Tradition (Richards), 39

Garden Cities, 55, 159, 188, 226, 232, 235, 237, 239
Geddes, Patrick, 25
Gibbs, James, *146*
Gibson Girl, 197
Giedion, S., 261
Gilbert, W.S., 16
Giles, J., *155*
Gimson, Ernest, 178, 188–9, *188*, *192*, 199; furniture of, 189, *190*, *191*
Girtin, T., 46
Gladstone, H.J., 241
Glasgow, 31, 34, 199, 200, 201, 234; Caledonian Road, Free Church, *149*; City Chambers, *157*; Cranston's Tea Rooms, Ingram St, 201, *202*; Main

St (No. 120), *200*; Moray Place, *151*; School of Art, 201–3, *204*, *205*
Godwin, E.W., 206, 234
Goebbels, Dr, 248
Goethe, W., 50
Goodhardt-Rendell, H.S., 15, 100, 158, 237
Goodhue, Bertram, 252
Gothic, 42, 59–64, 68, 79 *passim*; sham follies and ruins, 42, 53, 63, 65–6, *66*, 68, *69*, 72
Gothic Furniture, 211, 213, *214*
Gothic novel, 65, 68, 214
Gothic Architecture Improved (Batty Langley), 66
Gothic Revival, 35, 45, 48, 57, 59, 62, 64–109 *passim*
Gothic Revival, The (Clark), 15
Gothick, 67, 210
Grand Hotel, Scarborough, *154*
Gray, Thomas: poems illustrated by Bentley, *67*, 68
Great Day of His Wrath (Martin), *49*
Great Exhibition 1851, 31, 92, 111–13, 123–30, 158, 177, 184, 237, 243
Great Stove, Chatsworth, 126, *127*
Greville House, Chipping Campden, 213
Gribble, H., *163*
Gropius, Walter, 176, 178, 182, 184, 203, 235, 244, 246–52, *246*, *249*, 261
Grosvenor House, London, 216
Guaranty Building, Chicago, *259*

Hagen, 247
Hagley, Worcs., 65, *66*
Halles des Machines, Paris, 131, 135
Hamilton, Thomas, *150*
Hampstead, Ellerdale Road, 229
Hampton Court, 66
Hansom, J., 152
Hardwick, Philip, 94, 147, *147*
Hardy, Thomas, 17, 56
Harewood, Yorks., 219, 238
Harlaxton, Lincs., 214
Harrods, London, 148
Hartford, Conn., 102
Hartley, Jesse, *31*
Harvard, U.S.A., 251

Hawkshaw, J., *120*
Heal, Ambrose, 178, 189
Heal's, Tottenham Court Road, London, 189
Heathcote, Ilkley, Yorks., 232
Heine, H., 44
Herrenvolk, 113, 251
Highclere, Hants, 216
Highgate Cemetery, *168*
High Victorianism, 18, 93, 102, 136, 137, 143, 147, 148–69, 185, 187, *217*, 219, 225
Hill House, Helensburgh, 201
Hitchcock, Henry Russell, 201
Hoar Cross, Staffs., *108*
Holman Hunt, William, 185
Holmes, Sherlock, and Dr Watson, 153
Holyhead Road, 36, 118
Homestead, Frinton, Essex, *194*
Horta, Victor, 192, *194*, 199
Houses of Parliament, 19, 46, 63, 75, *75*, 77, *84*, *85*, 84–5, *86*, *87*, 98, 136–7, 153, 164
Huddleston, Baron, 98
Hugo, Victor, 59, 255
Hyde Park, London, *40*, 94, 116

Ibsen, H., 197
Ilkley, Yorks., 232
Impressionism, 187, 247
Imperial Institute, S. Kensington, 164, *165*
Industrial Revolution, 25–40, 113 *passim*, 207, 242 *passim*; Eotechnic, 25, 26, 27, 28, 30; Paleotechnic, 25, 26, 27, 28, 33, 243; Neotechnic, 25, 26
Inwood, Sir Henry, 143
Iron and Coal (Bell Scott), 51, 123

Jackson, T. G., *107*
James, Henry, 170, 251
Jekyll, Gertrude, *221*, 234
Jenkins, Frank, 186
Johnson, Dr S., 45, 47
Jones, Inigo, 19, 60, 62, 207
Jugendstil, 197

Kandinsky, W., 248

Kaufmann House, Bear Run, 260
Keats, J., 46
Keble, J., 46, 86
Keble College Chapel, 89, 90, *90*
Kelmscott Press, 175, 177, 180
Kemp, G. M., *105*
Kennington model, tenements, 237
Kensington, 93; Addison Road, *33*; Alford House, *212*; Gardens, 94, 116, 158; Gore, 92; Lowther Lodge, 229; Melbury Road (No. 9), 102, *103*; Queen's Gate, *228*; South Kensington, 18, 158–62, *161*, 164
Kent, William, 47
Kew, Palm House, 126, *127*
Killymoon, Co. Tyrone, 211
King Edward, 230
King's Cross Station, London, *117*, 131, *132*
Kinmell Park, Wales, 226
Kipling, Rudyard, 164, 256
Klee, Paul, 248
Knightley, T. E., *22*
Kropotkin, P., 255

Langham Hotel, London, 148, *155*
L'Architecture moderne en Angletere (Sédille), 192
Law Courts, Birmingham, 164
Law Courts, Strand, 75, 97, 98–101, *99*, *100*, *101*, 102, 137, 152–3
Lea Cottage, Charnwood, *188*
Leeds, 34; Town Hall, 152, *156*
Letchworth Garden City, 237
Lethaby, W. R., *91*, *160*, 219, 234, 255
Leys, The, Elstree, *196*
Leys Wood, nr Groombridge, Surrey, 226, 229
Life Guards, London, 74
Lilia Victoria Regia, 128
Liverpool, 29, 34, 40, 46, 148, 242; Albert Docks, *31*, 126; Bank of England, *145*, 147; Cathedral (Anglican), 97, 243; Cathedral (Roman Catholic), 235; Lime St Station, 143; St George's Hall, *140*, *141*, 143, 147, 152, 164
Locke, J., 35, 47

London Board Schools, 153
London County Council, 153, 158, *160*, 237, 238
Longhena, P., 171
Longleat, Wilts., 27, 60
Lorraine, Claude, 52
Lorrimer, Sir Edward, 214
Lowther Lodge, Kensington, 229
Lucas, F.L., 44
Lutyens, Edwin, 81, 178, 181, 190, 211, 216, 219, 224, 225, 226, 232, 233, 234–7, *235*, 256

Mackintosh, C.R., 194, 199–205, *200*, *202*, *204*, *205*, 234, 244
Maillart, Robert, 260
Mallet-Stephens, R., 201
Malory, Sir T., 62
Manchester, 18, 27, 29, 34, 35, 40, 46, 153; Assize Courts, *158*; Free Trade Hall, 152; Town Hall, 152, *159*; warehouses, *38*
Manchester philosophy, 113, 153
March, Phillips de Lisle, 78, 84
MARS Group, 233, 256
Marshall Field Store, Chicago, *253*
Martin, John, *49*, 122–3
Marx, Karl, 177, 241
McKim, Mead and White, 252
Melbury Road, Kensington (No. 9), 102, *103*
Merton, Morris Dye Works, 180
Metropolitan Railway, London, 33
Mettallic, 131
Mewès, C.F. and Davis, A.J., 230
Meyer, Adolf and Gropius, W., *246*, *249*
Michelangelo, 60
Mickle, William, 63
Midland Railway, 94, 128
Mies van der Rohe, Ludwig, 244
Millais, Sir J., 89, 93, *173*
Millbank, London, 153, *160*
Miller, Sanderson, 65, *66*
Milton, John, 62
Mimram Viaduct, Welwyn, *117*
Minton Tiles, 81, *88*, 90
Modern Painters (Ruskin), 56, 171, 172
Moholy-Nagy, L., 248

Morris, Jane, 198
Morris, William, 16, 46, 48, 71, 79, 92, 105, 122, 136, 166, 175, 176–84, *181*, *182*, 185, 186–7, 188, 189, 191, 192, 197, 199, 224, 226, 234, 241, 243, 244, 248, 250, 255, 258
Morris and Co., 177, 178
Mumford, Lewis, 25
Munich, 247
Municipal Building, New York, 252
Munstead Wood, Surrey, 234, *235*
Museum of modern art, Hagen, 247
Muthesius, Herman, 178, 192

Nash, John, *32*, 53, *53*, *54*, 55, 68, 72, 74, 78, 110, 116, 126, *139*, 140, *142*, 143, 148, 207–8, 211, *220*, 238
Nasmyth, J., 116
National Gallery, Berlin, 247
National Gallery, London, 74, 98, *146*, 147
Natural History Museum, London, 162
Nature of Gothic (Ruskin), 175–6
Neilson, J.B., 28
Nervi, P.L., 242, 260
Nesfield, Eden, 219, 226, 229
Newberry, Fra, 201
Newcastle upon Tyne, workers' cottages, *114*; Central Station, 126
New Delhi, 235
Newman, Cardinal, 46, 56, 78, *163*
News from Nowhere (Morris), 122, 177, 185
New York, 34; Municipal Building, 252; Pennsylvania Station, 252
New Zealand Chambers, London, 229, *229*
Nightingale, Florence, 51

Oak Hill Park Unity Church, 258, 260
Orchard, The, Chorley Wood, 191
Ordish, R.M., *128*
Osborne House, I.O.W., 43, *43*, *212*, 240
Ostberg, R., 178
Ouida, *155*

Oxford, 116, 171, 177; Banbury Road Houses, *236*; Brasenose College, *107*; Christ Church College, 62, 65; Keble College Chapel, 89, 90, *90*; Museum, *106*, 131, *134*, 135, 187; Taylorian Institute, 147; University, 207

Paddington Station, London, 118, *119*, 131
Palace of Westminster, 71, 74–6, 79, 84, 143, 209, 216
Palmer, Samuel, 46
Palmerston, Lord, 92
Palm House, Kew, 126, *127*
Papillon Hall, Leics., 234
Paris, 50, *53*, 126, *154*; *Halles des Machines*, 131; St Eugene, 131, 187
Paris Exhibition 1878, 197
Paris Exhibition 1889, 131, 197
Past and Present (Carlyle), 122, 178, 185, 255
Pater, W., 46
Paxton, Joseph, 55, *123*, *124*, *125*, 126–31, *127*, *129*, 221, 238–9
Payne Knight, *221*
Peabody Trust, 239, *239*
Pearson, J.L., *107*, *108*
Pembroke, Lord, 207
Pennsylvania Station, New York, 252
Perrycroft, Malvern, 190
Pevsner, Nikolaus, 15, 176, 244; on Gimson, 189; on Morris, 182; on Piccadilly Hotel, 232
Piccadilly Hotel, London, *231*, 232
Pickwick (Dickens), 35
Pioneers of the Modern Movement (Pevsner), 15, 176, 244
Porden, W., *53*
Portman, Duke of, 225, 232
Port Sunlight, Cheshire, 55
Poussin, N., 52
Praeterita (Ruskin), 174
Pre-Raphaelites, 45, 46, 48, 89, 93, 105, 111, 122, 171, 187, 198, 201, 209
Price, Uvedale, 53
Proust, Marcel, 55
Prudential Insurance Building, Holborn, 162

Pugin, A.W.N., 46, 71, *75*, 77–87, *77*, *79*, *80*, *82*, *83*, *84*, *85*, *86*, *87*, 97, 98, 102, 122, 136, 138, 148, *163*, 166, 176, 178, 180, 182, 186, 210, 213, 215, 216, 226, 244; and Barry, C., 84–5
Punch, 208
Pusey, E., 209
Puseyites, 111, 153, 210

Queen's Gate, Kensington (No. 185), *228*

Railway Age, The, 242, 261
Railway Station (Frith), *119*
Rain, Steam and Speed (Turner), 123
Reade, Wynwood, 255
Red House, Kent, 177, 178–82, *179*, 185, 188, 190, 224, 226; the settle, *182*
Reform Bill, 35, 39, 49, 76
Reform Club, London, 84, 215, 216, 219
Regent St, London, 15, 110
Regent's Park, London, 53, 113, 140,159
Renaissance, The, 26, 43, 58–9, 60, 116, 176, 178, 240, 255
Repton, Humphrey, 53
Richards, J.M., 39
Richardson, H.H., *253*
Rickman, Thomas, 136
Risorgimento, 51
Ritz Hotel, London, *154*, 230
Robertson, J., 55
Robie House, Chicago, 260
Romantic Movement, 42–57, 152, 170, 171, 177, 207, 255; and Imagination, 47–8; and Nature, 51–2, 55
Rome, 45, 58, 59, 63, 78, 148; Olympic Stadium, 242
Ronchamp, 45, 243
Rosetti, C., 46
Rosetti, D.G., 56, 198, 201
Roslin Castle, Midlothian, 63
Rousseau, J.J., 51
Royal Academy, 56, 110, 164, 208
Royal Albert Bridge, Saltash, *37*
Royal Courts of Justice, Strand, 75, 97, 98–100, *99*, *100*, *101*, 102, 137, 152–3
Royal Crescent, Bath, 46
Royal Exchange, London, 74, 147

Royal Holloway College, *217*, *218*
Royal Institute of British Architects, 110, 185–6
Royal Naval College, Dartmouth, 164
Royal Train, Queen Victoria's saloon, *121*
Ruines, en meditations sur les revolutions des Empires, Les (de Volney), 63
Ruskin, John, 40, 46, 48, 55–6, 71, 89, *106*, 111, 122, 135, 136, 170–6, 178, 180, 187, 192, 209, 244, 255
Ruskin, John (Millais), *173*

St Augustine's, Kilburn, *107*
St Chad's Cathedral, Birmingham, 81, *82*
St Cyprian's, Clarence Gate, *109*
St Eugène, Paris, 131, 187
St George's Hall, Liverpool, *140*, *141*, 143, 147, 152, 164
St James's Park, London, *53*, 74, *167*
St John's College, Cambridge, 62
St Katherine's Dock, London, *38*
St Luke's, Chelsea, 72, *73*
St Mark's, Venice, and Ruskin, 56, 171, 172–4, 176
St Mary Aldermary, London, *61*
St Mary's, Warwick, 62, 65
St Pancras Church, London, 143
St Pancras Hotel, 20, 94, *96*, 97, 137
St Pancras Station, 94, 111, 126, *128*
St Paul's, London, 18, 61
St Paul's School, Hammersmith, 162
St Peter's, Brighton, 72
St Saviour's Vicarage, Coalpit Heath, *91*
Salisbury, 176, 208
Saltash, Royal Albert Bridge, *37*
Salvin, Anthony, 214, 216
Santa Maria della Salute, Venice, 171
Savage, James, 72, *73*
Scarborough, Grand Hotel, *154*
Scarisbrick, Charles, 78, 79, 210
Scarisbrick Hall, 79–81, *79*, *80*, 84, 180, 213
Scott, Bell, 51, 123
Scott, Sir Gilbert, 46, 92–7, *95*, *96*, 98, 100, 135, 137, 138, 148, *167*, 187, 280

Scott, Giles, 97
Scott, Sir Walter, 40, 46, 116, 214
Scott Memorial, Edinburgh, 93, *105*
School for Scandal (Sheridan), 47
Scuola san Rocco, 172
Seaton Delaval, Northumberland, 61
Sédille, Paul, 192
Seven Lamps of Architecture (Ruskin), 93, 122
Shackelford, Surrey, *193*
Shaftesbury, Lord, 51
Shakespeare, W., 60, 62
Shaw, G.B., 197, 235
Shaw, Norman, 81, 138, *179*, 181, 219, 224–34, *225*, *227*, *228*, *229*, *230*, *231*, *232*, 234
Sheerness Boat Sheds, *242*
Sheffield, 19, 34
Shelley, P.B., 46, 51, 63, 255
Shrewsbury, Earl of, 78, 81, 208, 210
Shrubland, Norfolk, 219
Siddal, Elizabeth, 198
Smiles, Samuel, 94, 241
Smirke, Sir Robert, 72, 143, *144*, 147, 148
Smith, William, *215*
Soane, Sir John, 59, 60, 68, 72, 116, 126, 148, 152
Socialist League, 177
Society for the protection of ancient buildings, 16, 189
Somerset House, London, 152
Stafford House, London, 216, 219, *221*
Stand, Lancs., 72
Statham, Heathcote, 97
Stephenson, R., 35, *118*
Stile Liberty, 197
Stockholm, Town Hall, 178
Stockport, viaduct and canal, *30*, 122
Stones of Venice (Ruskin), 46, 48, 56, *106*, 111, 135, *173*, 172–6, 185
Stowe, Bucks., 140
Strachey, Lytton, 94
Strawberry Hill, Twickenham, *64*, *65*, 65–8, 81, 140, 209
Street, George Edward, 97–101, *99*, *100*, *101*, 102, 136, 138, 152–3, 176
Stroud Valley Mills, 34

Studio, 195
Sullivan, Louis, 135, 199, 247, 252–5, *254*, 256, *257*, 258, *259*
Summerson, Sir John, 89, 203
Sun of Venice Going to Sea (Turner), 122
Swan House, Chelsea, 229–30, *230*
Swinburne, A.C., 197, 198
Sycamore Road, Bourneville, *238*
Sylva (Evelyn), 52

Talbert, Bruce, *195*
Taylorian Institute, Oxford, 147
Technics and Civilization (Mumford), 25
Telford, Thomas, 36, *38*, 116
Tempest, The (Shakespeare), 52
Temple of Jupiter Stator, Birmingham, 152
Temple Meads Station, Bristol, 118
Temple Moore, 105
Tennyson, Lord A., 40, 46
Thackeray, W.M., 56, 113
Thermae, 153
Thermae of Caracalla, 143
Thomson, Alexander, *149*, *151*
Thoreau, H.D., 233
Tintoretto, 172, 174
Tolstoy, A., 255
Tower Bridge, London, *32*
Town Hall, Leeds, 152, *156*
Town Hall, Manchester, 18, 152, *159*
Town Hall, Stockholm, 178
Trabeated, 131
Tractarian Movement, 17, 62, 72, 122, 177
Trafalgar Square, London, *146*, 147
Travellers' Club, London, 84, 215
Trentham Hall, 219, *221*
Trinity College, Hartford, Conn., 102
Trollope, A., 17
Truro Cathedral, *108*
Turner, J.M.W., 45, 46, 55, 56, *119*, 122, 123, 171
Turner, Richard, *127*

University, Birmingham, 164
University College, London, 147
University Museum, Oxford, *106*, 131, *134*, 135

Unto This Last (Ruskin), 175–6, 178, 185

Vanburgh, Sir J., 61, 207
Van der Velde, H., 191, 192, 199, 247
Venice, 26, 40; and Ruskin, 171–5, 176
Victoria and Albert Museum, 162, *162*
Victoria Embankment, *122*
Victoria Fountain, 164
Victoria, Queen, 19, 29, 33, *43*, 43–4, 60, 111, *121*, 126, 136–7, 206, 219, 240
Victorian Architectural Professions, The (Jenkins), 186
Victorian, Early, 92, 147, 148
Victorian, High, 136–69, 243
Victorian houses, 206–37, *236*; housing, 237–9, *238*, *239*
Victorian patronage, 209–10, 224
Victorian Society, The, 16
Vienna, 50, *53*; Secessionist Exhibition, 201, 203
Viollet-le-Duc, E., 135, 187
Voltaire, F., 50, 51
Voysey, C.F.A., 178, *179*, 189–91, *193*, *194*, 197, 199, 201, 219, 226, 233–4, 244

Wainwright Building, St Louis, 252, 258
Wallington Hall, Northumberland, 123
Walpole, Horace, 42, 65–8, 71, 72, 79
Walter, Edward, 152
Walton, George, *196*
Wandsworth Prison, London, *41*
Warehouses, Manchester, *38*
Waterhouse, Alfred, 18, 27, 97, 98, 100, 152, 153, *158*, *159*, 162, 219, *222*, *223*
Watson, Dr, and Sherlock Holmes, 153
Watt, J., 35, 40
Waverley (Scott), 68, 93, 214
Webb, Sir Aston, *53*, 162, 164, 187
Webb, Philip, *91*, 105, 178–81, *179*, *183*, 185, 188, 190, 199, 209, 219, 224, 226, 229, 233, 234
Weimar, 50, 209, 214, 247
Weimar Academy, 248
Weimar Bauhaus, 248
Welsh, Jane, 113

Welwyn Garden City, 237
Werkbund Exhibition Factory, Cologne, *249*
Werkbund, The, 247
Westminster Hall, 74, 98
Westminster *see* Houses of Parliament and Palace of Westminster
Whistler, J. McNeill, 197, 206, 234
Whitehall Court, London, 18, 74, 152
White House, Leics., *192*
White House, Tite St, Chelsea, 206, 234
Whitman, Walt, 233, 251, 252, 255, 256
Wilberforce, W., 51
Wilde, Oscar, 197, 198, 199
Wilkins, William, 143, *146*, 147
Wilton House, Wilts., 62, 207, 210
Windsor, 43, 68, 140
Windy Hill, Kilmacolm, 201
Wollaton Hall, 60

Woodward, B., and Deane, Sir T., *106*, 131, *134*, 135
Wordsworth, 46, 51, 55, 56, 122, 255
Work (Brown), *112*, 113
Wren, Sir Christopher, 55, 60, 61, *61*, 62, 89, 98
Wright, Frank Lloyd, 27, 135, 182, 184, 211, 233, 235, 244, 247, 251, 252, 255–60, 261
Wuthering Heights (Brontë), 46
Wyatt, Benjamin, 219
Wyatt, James, 68, *69*, *70*, 71–2, 138, 182, 206, 210, 211
Wyatt, M. Digby, 131, *212*

Yeats, W. B., 45, 176, 177
Yellow Book, 198, 199, 203, 232, 234
Yonge, Charlotte, 46
Young, G. M., 17
Young, J., *142*
Young, W., *157*

Some other books published by Penguins on subjects
of related interest are described on the following
pages.

A PEREGRINE BOOK

THE ENGLISHNESS OF ENGLISH ART

Nikolaus Pevsner

No one is better qualified than Professor Pevsner to under-
take this discussion of national characteristics in English art.
Born and educated on the Continent, he has the unbiased eye
of the foreigner, and having lived and worked in England for
over thirty years he possesses an unrivalled knowledge of his
subject.

To draw the contours of this 'geography of art' it is necessary, says the author, to look at matters in terms of 'polarities', since it is only in examining the seeming contradictions
of art that we can hope to discover what is specifically English in each distinctive style.

Two such polarities are the Decorated and the Perpendicu_
lar styles in architecture – the one all undulating curves and
playful spatial rhythms, the other relying entirely on the
straight line for its effect of uninterrupted spatial clarity.
And yet, in that both are anti-corporeal, denying volume any
part in the performance, both are unmistakably English.

This well-illustrated survey of English visual and functional art was described, in its original form, by the *Journal
of Education* as being 'far and away the best of the Reith
Lectures so far'.

PIONEERS OF MODERN DESIGN

Nikolaus Pevsner

From William Morris to Walter Gropius

The history of the Modern Movement in architecture and design was an almost unknown field until Nikolaus Pevsner first published his *Pioneers* in 1936. This soon came to be recognized as the standard work on the subject and was revised and enlarged in 1949 and has been again revised and partly rewritten for this Pelican edition.

Professor Pevsner tells the exciting story of how the efforts of a relatively small group of men lifted our visual concepts away from stale Victorian Historicism and infused them once more with honesty, fitness of purpose, and contemporary expression. He shows how the foundation of the best that surrounds us today was laid then by men who thought and taught as well as designed.

GEORGIAN LONDON

John Summerson

George I came to the throne in 1714; George IV died in 1830. Between those dates Georgian London transformed itself into a great Imperial Capital. A criss-cross pattern of streets and squares covered former marshes and meadows; new bridges spanned the Thames at Westminster and Blackfriars, and later at three more points; new roads linked Paddington and Islington, and pushed down into Southwark and Lambeth; villages such as Hackney and Fulham became suburbs; and the arcaded terraces of Somerset House and the Adelphi hinted at a Thames Embankment. These are some of the bare facts of the development: in *Georgian London* Sir John Summerson fills them with life and meaning, showing how closely the buildings and the history of an age are connected. Statesmen, connoisseurs, merchants, architects, and jerrybuilders – all are characters in this absorbing story.

'The title gives no idea of the variety and scope, the interest and entertainment, of this learned and lively book. It treats not only of Georgian architecture, but of the whole problem of the growth of a city' – *Times Literary Supplement.*

'As interesting as it is erudite' – *New Statesman.*

THE GOTHIC REVIVAL

Kenneth Clark

Few movements in the history of art and taste have been so derided as the Gothic Revival. In this lively study – a new edition of his first book – Sir Kenneth Clark examines the Gothic Revival with highly critical sympathy. He traces the neo-Gothic impulse from its origins in eighteenth-century literature through the pseudo-medieval houses and follies to the Oxford Movement, Gilbert Scott, and Ruskin, all of whom receive detailed attention.

He reminds us of the movement's successes as well as its notorious failures. If Walpole's Strawberry Hill is mere quaintness, and if many of Scott's church restorations were indefensible, the Gothic Revival did produce Pugin, Butterfield, and Street, and would be remembered by every visitor to London for the Houses of Parliament alone.

'Sympathetic but discerning treatment of a mainly English phenomenon' – *The Times Literary Supplement.*

ENGLISH FURNITURE STYLES
1500–1830

Ralph Fastnedge

This is a comprehensive, compact, and authoritative historical survey of the evolution of English furniture. In recent years interest in its makers has been growing. Legends have been dispelled, and new facts and material correlated, so that our knowledge of the history of furniture design is now very much more exact. Chippendale, Hepplewhite, and Sheraton, for example, are seen no longer as fabulous, isolated figures, but in true perspective; and their famous pattern books (the *Director*, the *Guide*, and the *Drawing Book*), which have been known to collectors for many years, have been studied very closely. Quotations from old memoirs, diaries, and letters, which are often entertaining and very illuminating, help to re-create the social conditions under which the designers and makers were working. The book has several useful appendices, including glossaries of makers, woods, and specialized terms, and is illustrated by over 200 line drawings and 64 pages of plates.

THE FUTURE OF LONDON

Edward Carter

The Future of London is unique among town-planning books. It is both exciting to read and authoritative in content. It shows vividly that the factors underlying any plan – land-values, traffic, housing and social facilities, open spaces, skyscrapers, and the aesthetic quality of what is built – are something of vital concern to every city-dweller, for they will determine the pattern of his life in the future.

A city is not just a mass of concrete, steel, bricks, and asphalt. It is also a place where thousands or millions of people are born and brought up, work and play, grow old and die. A modern capital must provide the conditions in which its inhabitants can lead full, happy, and healthy lives.

In this fascinating discussion of the decay and renewal of the Metropolis, the Director of the Architectural Association looks at the different plans, past and present, that exist for its development. He shows that the need for action is urgent, for with every year of unplanned chaos the problems grow more intractably.

It is for us to decide whether tomorrow's London will be an uninhabitable jungle or a capital to be proud of.

A HISTORY OF LONDON LIFE

R. J. Mitchell and M. D. R. Leys

We have all heard of the Great Fire of 1666, but how many of us know of the Great Stink of 1858? The 'Blind Beak', Bartholomew Fair, public executions, the street vendors of birds' nests, groundsel, and lavender – these and many other curiosities are all described in this intriguing chronicle of the lives of London's inhabitants, ranging in time from pre-Roman days to the formation of the L.C.C. The authors, both distinguished historians, have drawn on varied contemporary sources such as unpublished letters, official documents, cartoons, and advertisements, to present an unusual and entertaining survey. Each of the chapters is linked with the name of a famous Londoner representative of his age, and through the eyes of such as Chaucer, the Chippendales, and Charles Dickens a fascinating composite picture of the metropolis emerges.

'Provides much welcome information, and is equipped with model footnotes to indicate sources. Sections cover every possible interest' – *Daily Telegraph*.

ENGLAND IN THE NINETEENTH CENTURY

David Thomson

The theme of this book is the major social changes which the people of England experienced during the period of 'the great peace' between the Battle of Waterloo and the First World War. Political, economic, intellectual, diplomatic, and other 'specialized' forms of history are drawn upon only in so far as they help to illuminate the changes in mental habit or outlook, or in social life and organization, which make up the story of the development of the English nation in that century. The underlying motif is the remarkable accumulation of material wealth and power which the English people achieved, and this is the story of whence it derived, how it was used, and how it eventually diminished.

It was an age when the English exported everything in abundance – men and ideas, as well as money and goods. At a time when production and exports are our major economic problem, it may be that we can find wisdom in the experience of Victorian England.